W9-CPB-930

CC2017

Lakes

Jeanne K. Hanson

Foreword by
Geoffrey H. Nash, Geologist

CHELSEA HOUSE
PUBLISHERS
An imprint of Infobase Publishing

LAKES

Chelsea House
An imprint of Infobase Publishing
132 West 31st Street
New York NY 10001

ISBN-10: 0-8160-5914-4
ISBN-13: 978-0-8160-5914-0

Library of Congress Cataloging-in-Publication Data
Hanson, Jeanne K.
    Lakes / Jeanne K. Hanson; foreword, Geoffrey H. Nash.
        p. cm. — (The extreme earth)
    Includes bibliographical references (p.) and index.
    ISBN 0-8160-5914-4
    1. Lakes. I. Title: 10 of the most unusual lakes. II. Title. III. Series.
    GB1603.7.H36 2007
    551.48'2—dc22
    2005034327

Chelsea House books are available at special discounts when purchased in bulk quantities for businesses, associations, institutions, or sales promotions. Please call our Special Sales Department in New York at (212) 967-8800 or (800) 322-8755.

You can find Chelsea House on the World Wide Web at
http://www.chelseahouse.com

Text design by Erika K. Arroyo
Cover design by Dorothy M. Preston/Salvatore Luongo
Illustrations by Melissa Ericksen
Photo research by Diane K. French

Printed in the United States of America

FOF VB 10 9 8 7 6 5 4 3 2 1

This book is printed on acid-free paper.

Contents

Foreword

Lakes are not static geologic features, frozen in time and changeless; they are dynamic and changing, because of local and global influences that are both natural and human-made. Geology is not just a study of the past. We are currently living in the geologic age called the Holocene, the most recent of the geologic ages that mark the 4.5 billion years since the Earth was formed. Even the oldest lakes are young in comparison to the age of the Earth because the inexorable forces of plate tectonics pushing the continents in continuous motion have altered the surface of the planet dramatically.

Lakes, by Jeanne Hanson, presents 10 examples of unusual lakes formed by the powerful forces of tectonic activity, glaciers, volcanism, and other agents. Depending on where you live, you may be lucky enough to be within an easy drive of some of these lakes that you can visit. When you go to these or other lakes, you will be more aware of the complexity lying just below the waves. In a world whose surface is dominated by salty oceans, freshwater is rare and worth appreciating, studying, and protecting. All this can start with understanding how lakes develop, age, and even disappear. With some basic information about these superlative lake examples, you can even apply your knowledge to a small pond in a nearby park.

Readers will be familiar with several of the lakes discussed in this book:

- Lake Superior, one of the Great Lakes in the United States
- Crater Lake, located inside a volcano crater
- the Great Salt Lake, saltier than the ocean

Other lakes discussed in this volume may not be as well known:

- the Caspian Sea, salty like a "sea" but really a lake
- Lake Baikal, the world's oldest lake, and biggest by volume
- Lake Eyre, a body of water that sometimes disappears, then "reappears."

Characteristics that relate these lakes to one another are their relative recent formation and their rarity as bodies of freshwater. Differences between lakes arise from their respective size, depth, local geology, biology, climate, and human impacts to which they are each subject. All lakes are affected by these influences and respond to them eventually. No lake stays the same for long if you are looking at it from the perspective of the geologic timescale.

Two recurring features of this book are the "In the Field" sections that detail field methods used by geologists like me to study lakes and the author's insights into areas of study where future scientists may wish to research further. May this type of focus spark the reader's awareness and interest in the natural sciences and lead to further contributions to the field. By taking a "world tour" within the pages of this book, you will also gain an appreciation of geography because these lakes are scattered all over the planet.

Lakes can be used as a detailed but accessible reference to understand lake processes and also as a readable entry point into the connectedness of all of the natural sciences. A reference list is also included for those who wish to investigate the topic further. You never know where the search will take you.

—Geoffrey H. Nash, Geologist

Preface

From outer space, Earth resembles a fragile blue marble, as revealed in the famous photograph taken by the *Apollo 17* astronauts in December 1972. Eugene Cernan, Ronald Evans, and Jack Schmitt were some 28,000 miles (45,061 km) away when one of them snapped the famous picture that provided the first clear image of the planet from space.

Zoom in closer and the view is quite different. Far beneath the vast seas that give the blue marble its rich hue are soaring mountains and deep ridges. On land, more mountains and canyons come into view, rugged terrain initiated by movement beneath the Earth's crust and then sculpted by wind and water. Arid deserts and hollow caves are here too, existing in counterpoint to coursing rivers, sprawling lakes, and plummeting waterfalls.

The Extreme Earth is a set of eight books that presents the geology of these landforms, with clear explanations of their origins, histories, and structures. Similarities exist, of course, among the many mountains of the world, just as they exist among individual rivers, caves, deserts, canyons, waterfalls, lakes, ocean ridges, and trenches. Some qualify as the biggest, highest, deepest, longest, widest, oldest, or most unusual, and these are the examples singled out in this set. Each book introduces 10 superlative examples, one by one, of the individual landforms, and reveals why these landforms are never static, but always changing. Some of them are internationally known, located in populated areas. Others are in more remote locations and known primarily to people in the region. All of them are worthy of inclusion.

To some people, the ever-shifting contours of the Earth are just so much scenery. Others sit and ponder ocean ridges and undersea trenches, imagining mysteries that they can neither interact with nor examine in person. Some gaze at majestic canyons, rushing waterfalls, or placid lakes, appreciating the scenery from behind a railing, on a path, or aboard a boat. Still others climb mountains, float rivers, explore caves, and cross deserts, interacting directly with nature in a personal way.

Even people with a heightened interest in the scenic wonders of the world do not always understand the complexity of these landforms. The eight books in the Extreme Earth set provide basic information on how individual landforms came to exist and their place in the history of the planet. Here, too, is information on what makes each one unusual, what roles they play in the world today, and, in some cases, who discovered and named them. Each chapter in each volume also includes material on environmental challenges and reports on science in action, with details on field studies conducted at each site. All the books include photographs in color and black-and-white, line drawings, a glossary of scientific terms related to the text, and a listing of resources for more information.

When students who have read the eight books in the Extreme Earth set venture outdoors—whether close to home, on a family vacation, or to distant shores—they will know what they are looking at, how it got there, and what likely will happen next. They will know the stories of how lakes form, how wind and weather work together to etch mountain ranges, and how water carves canyons. These all are thrilling stories—stories that inhabitants of this planet have a responsibility to know.

The primary goal of the Extreme Earth set of books is to inform readers of all ages about the most interesting mountains, rivers, caves, deserts, canyons, waterfalls, lakes, ocean ridges, and trenches in the world. Even as these books serve to increase both understanding of the history of the planet and appreciation for all its landforms, ideally they also will encourage a sense of responsible stewardship for this magnificent blue marble.

Acknowledgments

I would like to thank Frank K. Darmstadt, executive editor, for his skillful guidance, Diane French, for her expertise as a photo researcher, and the rest of the editorial and production staff for their invaluable contributions.

Introduction

*L*akes is written as a science tour of the world for readers. It is time travel, too, unreeling the earth history of each of the 10 lakes featured by explaining what was there before the lake, how it formed, how it has changed, and why. It can be interesting to know what is found underfoot, by the side of the road, part of an outdoor vacation, or otherwise encountered.

The 10 lakes range from a giant saltwater lake (the Caspian Sea) to a polluted and shrinking lake (the Aral Sea), from the most extensive lake (Lake Superior) to the lake with the greatest volume of water (Lake Baikal), to the highest lake large enough to be navigable (Lake Titicaca). In yet more variety, the chapters go on to feature Europe's largest lake (Lake Vänern), a lake that sometimes vanishes (Lake Eyre), a lake that formed after a volcanic explosion (Crater Lake), a salty lake that can look pink (Great Salt Lake), and a subarctic lake (Great Slave Lake). In these ways, and more, the lakes chosen are extreme.

The lakes of this book are in the Middle East, the United States, Russia, South America, Europe, Australia, and Canada. Even more lakes, found elsewhere, are featured in some of the boxed "sidebars" found in the chapters, including two lakes in Africa that explode, a lake in California that has turned to dangerous dust, and much more. The book is a world tour, at the level of the rocks.

Like the other books in this set, The Extreme Earth, this volume begins with the "Origins of the Landform," a short chapter that provides the framework, describing the main ways lakes form on this planet. If you read it before beginning the book and again before launching into each chapter, you will be able to place each lake in perspective, arranging the furniture of the mind well.

The book also features a bit of science-in-action. Each chapter includes at least one "In the Field" section, which tells how geologists are using various techniques to study that lake today. Readers who are considering geology as a profession might even go back after finishing the book to read all of these sections again—they are always at the end of the chapter—to get a beginning sense of the field.

One thing these books will not do: settle a bet. Does Lake Baikal hold exactly 14,000 cubic miles (58,355 km³) of water, or is the number found on some Web site or in some almanac the correct one? In researching this book it quickly became evident that almost every source offered different numbers for the lakes' dimensions. This is not because of carelessness or ignorance on the part of either the author or sources. More rain or less rain one year, or even one month, changes a lake's volume a bit. Even a lake's length and width change depending upon when and how those dimensions were measured. The beginning and ending dates for the various broad geological periods also differ among sources. In assembling the statistics for each lake in the book, we consulted many sources and here provide the best approximations possible.

Origin of
the Landform

Lakes

Viewed from space, our planet is blue and green, but mostly blue. More than 71 percent of the surface of the Earth is water, about 36 million cubic miles (150 km³) of it. Almost all of this—more than 97 percent—lies in the oceans as salt water. The remaining 3 percent, the freshwater, is composed of all of the groundwater (water flowing underground), the glaciers, the rivers, and the lakes of the world. This book focuses on the lakes.

Freshwater is rare, so rare across the planet that it could be considered blue gold. Without it, life on this planet would not exist. So it is useful to learn about lakes, beginning with a glimpse at the "big picture," the origin of this beautiful and important landform.

Though a lake may look as though it has existed forever, reflecting the sky and clouds in all their tones and shapes, this is not the case. The Earth is an unquiet planet, constantly being shaped in four main ways, naturally and slowly. The first is through the broad movements of huge *plates* of rooted rock. These thick pieces of the planet's *crust* move across the surface, gradually shifting the landmasses, and the lakes within them, as a giant 3-D puzzle.

Climate change over the ages is the second major force to shape the face of the planet and the lakes upon it. It causes glaciers to thicken and shove the land, then melt in immense volumes, rivers to rush fast enough over eons to sweep away hills and block valleys, frost to crack the rocks that make up the mountains until even the mountains tumble down. Perhaps amazingly, most of the major lakes of the world owe their existence to glaciers and their aftermath.

The third natural "engine" of our planet is *tectonic/igneous activity*, as exemplified by earthquakes and volcanoes. They crack, push, and pile up the land, or breathe out deep heat from underground that melts rock. Lakes can form in the shapes they create.

The fourth great shape-shifter, erosion, is actually the most significant of these forces of natural change, for the planet as a whole—and the trickiest. Its work often covers up evidence of the other three. Erosion can push up enough soil to make a river slide aside, raise hills that change where the snowmelt flows, and fill in valleys with sediments. All these forces set the stage for the creation, change, and elimination of lakes.

WHY?

The first and best questions about the natural world are always the whys and the hows. Why did a particular lake form where it did and how long ago? Why has it filled with water? Why is it changing, and what did it once look like? Why is one lake so much saltier than another? What is its water chemistry, its biological activity? How do heat, the shape of the lake's basin, light, the water's inflow and outflow affect the lake? How does a lake "turn over" in the spring and fall? How do changes in its oxygen, nitrogen, and other chemical levels change a lake? How is human activity altering the lake? Questions like these lead into geology, the study of the Earth across time. Lakes are part of its focus.

LAKE FORMATION

Lakes begin to form in 10 main ways, as described below, with some of these much more common in occurrence than others. The first, *tectonic forces*, can indeed form lakes, as slabs of rock are lifted up or made to slump, creating a new basin where water can collect. Secondly, volcanic forces create lakes, as lava erupts then collapses into a new basin or flows out to dam a river. Landslides, a third mechanism, can also form bodies of water, when a flood or earthquake moves enough rocky soil to dam a river. (Since this material is not as dense as rock, the dam often washes away in a few weeks or months, ending the life of this kind of lake relatively quickly.)

Glaciers, a fourth method of lake formation, has been, and is, very significant on our planet, especially in the *Pleistocene epoch* which began about 2 million years ago. These ice monsters both pressed the land down and scooped it out on a giant scale, creating the basins that we now know as the Great Lakes as well as many other lakes large and small. Glaciers acted just as powerfully when they melted. Even the Great Salt Lake began long ago with glacial meltwater.

Less common methods of lake formation—by solution, by river, by wind, by shoreline change, by organic activity, and by deliberate action— can also be important. One type of lake, a "solution lake," can form when groundwater or surface water dissolves rock, usually limestone, creating a small basin. Rivers also can create lakes, by blocking a valley, or changing their own course to fill a lowlands, for example. Wind forms lake basins, too, by piling up sand and gravel in which water can collect. (These lakes, though, are usually short-lived.) Shoreline changes also create lakes, when part of a larger lake or ocean becomes cut off from its main body of water.

Organic activity can even make lakes, especially when a great many plants die and form a dam behind which water collects; this is more in common in the tropics than in the temperate zones of the planet, and these lakes are usually not long-lived. The last method, lake formation by deliberate action of humans (with, believe it or not, the occasional contribution by only one other animal, the beaver) is increasingly common. This kind of activity can create reservoirs, or decorative artificial lakes, or forest pools. People are such champion land movers that our efforts displace more than 40 billion tons of soil and rock each year, in house construction, mining, and highway building alone; some of this serves to create lakes.

Of the natural methods of lake formation, only three create the larger, more varied, longer-lived lakes that will be the subject of this book: the tectonic forces, the volcanic forces, and the glaciers. These three earth forces are so powerful that it is estimated that the tectonic forces alone shove up about 14 billion tons of rock each year across the planet, forming mountains and cracking land in half across hundreds of miles to create both *rifts* and basins. Volcanoes worldwide raise about 30 billion tons of rock up from the ocean floor to make land in new places each year and explode on land to create *caldera* for lakes. And glaciers, the most significant force in lake creation of all, push about 4.3 billion tons of land around annually, even now. This effect is unimaginably less than what they accomplished in their most recent heyday just a few thousand years ago, when many lakes were made. A planet without these three energetic, dynamic forces would not have seen the creation of very many lakes. The Earth will reward all the curiosity one can summon to the understanding of these major engines of change.

A LAKE: HOW MUCH WATER?

Once a lake forms, it develops a "water economy," a balance of some kind in its inflow/outflow "budget." This involves several key factors. First, the inflow. Lakes receive their water from precipitation (rain and snowmelt), from ground flow (via runoff, rivers, and the like), and from groundwater seeping in. The pattern of inflow changes with both season and climate. It is also affected by the shape of the lake's basin, the nature of the runoff, the rivers, and groundwater, and by the lake's location on the planet. The position of the lake with regard to the ocean makes an especial difference, too, since lakes nearer to an ocean receive less rainfall; it rains more over land than over ocean worldwide, and more water evaporates from the ocean than from the land.

The outflow of water from a lake occurs in several ways. Evaporation and transpiration (plants consuming water) are key. Important also are flow over the surface (a river may draw water away from a lake) and seepage of water into the land groundwater (though lakes usually "leak" only near the shoreline).

Every water molecule, part of this in-and-out dance, can be thought of as having a "residence time" in which it moves through the system. A unit of water stays up in the atmosphere for an average of 8.9 days before it comes down as precipitation. It remains in a lake or river for an average of 6.6 years, in the ocean for an average of 3,060 years, in the glacial ice of Greenland for an average of 4,500 years, and in the frozen-solid silence of Antarctica for an average of 14,000 years. Even a planet whose landscape may seem to change little is dynamic in its water economy. A lake's water is changing all the time, even without human influence.

TEN LAKES

The 10 lakes chosen for this book—Caspian Sea, Aral Sea, Lake Superior, Lake Baikal, Lake Titicaca, Lake Vänern, Lake Eyre, Crater Lake, Great Salt Lake, and Great Slave Lake—are all large, varied, and interesting, and lie all around the world. One is the deepest, one the saltiest, one the highest, one the oldest, one holds the most water, one is changing the most, one is in the largest grouping of lakes, one is actually horrifying, and so on. Readers of this book will be able to find out which is which. Along the way the book provides sidebars about smaller but very interesting lakes, such as the one that exploded about 20 years ago. There will also be information about how geologists study lakes. Our blue planet is filled with surprises for those willing and able to think about what is around their feet or splashing at the dock.

Caspian Sea

Middle East

The Caspian Sea, the largest lake in the world, is about 144,000 square miles (375,000 km²) in extent, more than half the size of Texas. North to south, it stretches about 745 miles (1,199 km). The Caspian is also the most saline (the saltiest) lake on the planet. Ranging from 3 percent to 8 percent saline, it is almost half as salty as the ocean.

While the Caspian is called a "sea" because of its size, it is actually a lake, surrounded on all sides by these Middle Eastern countries: Kazakhstan, Azerbaijan, Georgia, Turkmenistan, and Iran. Once controlled by the Soviet Union, before that country broke up into republics in 1991, the Caspian lies east of the Black Sea and even farther east of the Mediterranean. The Black Sea and the Mediterranean Sea, unlike the Caspian, are both connected to the ocean.

At shore level in most places, this is an immense, hot, dry, salty place. It is ringed by low desert to the north, a higher desert plateau (called a grassy "steppe") to the east, the Caucasus Mountains not far to the west, and an area of cropland to the south where sugarcane, fruit, and other foods are grown. A huge desert lies just south of that zone. Desert is encroaching every year on the Caspian's southwest and south sides, a process called desertification. This land change generally results not only from poor rainfall but also from human practices that increase soil erosion or worsen soil quality, damaging the conditions plants need to grow (the unanchored topsoil then blows away). Sand dunes lie on parts of the Caspian's east and south shores. Shaped and changed by wave action and wind action, the southern dunes rise as high as 50 feet (15.24 m) above the Caspian.

GEOPOLITICS

The political position of the Caspian Sea is dramatic, too. Vast oil and natural gas reserves—geologic in origin—lie around its shores and under its waters. One of these, the Kashagan oil field, sprawls north and northeast of the lake in Kazakhstan, and is the largest area of oil discovery worldwide in

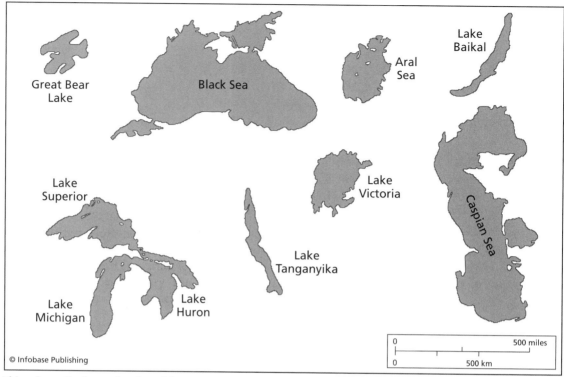

This schematic shows the size of the Caspian Sea in relation to selected other lakes and to the Black Sea, which is not a lake since it is connected to the Mediterranean.

nearly 50 years. This field should yield 13 billion barrels of oil, more even than Saudi Arabia's immense oil fields, once it becomes further developed. But for nearly 100 years already, oil has been pumped out of parts of the Caspian area.

All five of its border countries are vying for control of the Caspian's seabed (underwater) oil, and that makes geological study and exploration especially active here. Multinational oil companies are jockeying for position to exploit both this oil and the huge reserves of natural gas—and then to move it to the West through new pipelines they have been constructing. Western countries are among those involved, including the United States. This group has won the main pipeline route it wanted—across Georgia to Turkey—thus avoiding the transit of most of the Middle Eastern countries.

The Azerbaijani capital city of Baku, on the large Abseron peninsula jutting into the Caspian, is another rich area for lakebed oil, as well as an important nexus for terrorists from around the Middle East. Politics like these are called geopolitics because they emerge from the geography and geology of an area.

The Caspian's geology is unusually interesting not only because it has led to such *salinity*, but also because it is a place of *tectonic activity* that features major earthquakes, underwater volcanoes, and other seismic events (though no active volcanoes). The area is home, too, to the fossil fuels of oil and gas, whose exploitation is far more recent than the dramatic Earth-upheavals, which created the Caspian; these shall be discussed last.

LOW ELEVATION

The Caspian Sea lies within a vast, low area of the planet. Its water conceals two especially deep basins, which together hold about 60 percent of the water volume of the lake. One is part of the southern part of the lake, and the other in its central stretch. The deepest point in the lake is

This aerial view shows a winter scene at the Caspian, with mountains and a river delta. *(CORBIS)*

3,104 feet (946 m) down, more than half a mile. The two underwater basins are separated by an underwater area of higher seabed called a rill. The northern section of the lake is somewhat shallower and sometimes even partly freezes for short periods of time in winter.

The Caspian's shoreline is 98 feet (30 m) below sea level and 90 feet (27.5 m) below the level of the Baltic Sea, the section of the Atlantic Ocean between Sweden and Poland and Germany. This elevation is one of the lowest on the planet.

What has happened here to create this low basin is that the Earth's *crust* has slumped. The phenomenon is called a downfold or *syncline*, the result of rock layers being both bent down and compressed. The most common cause of a syncline is the formation of mountains nearby, and that is the situation here. The Caucasus Mountains, one of the most active mountain ranges on Earth, is still uplifting (growing higher) nearby. The Alps, the Urals, and the Himalayas are "near," too, geologically speaking. But the story really begins before that.

ORIGINS: FIRST STAGES

In the early days of Earth's history, this area was partly island and partly underwater—in an ancient ocean called the Tethys Sea. The life of the island lasted from about 650 million years ago to about 430 million years ago, overlapping with much of the early *Paleozoic epoch* (500 to 225 million years ago). Also during this period, the land that was to become the Ural Mountains (north of the present Caspian) began to change, first forming a deep trough that filled with sediments, then uplifting as rock masses shoved in underneath. The whole area was joined with what is now Siberia, making a large continental section. By that time the Caspian's area was no longer considered an island. The stretch of the present Caspian once under the Tethys Sea later absorbed salt when the sea dried out.

Though it happens in slow motion, everything on the planet moves around in ways like this. The process is called *plate tectonics*. The crust and *upper mantle* layers of the Earth are split into giant jigsaw puzzle pieces called *plates*. These plates are made of slabs of rock, which carry the lighter continents on their backs. The plates have probably been shifting around for as long as 3.5 billion years and will continue to do so into the future. As a result, no continent today is where it once was. Though research continues, geologists' best estimate is that there are seven major plates, eight medium ones, and about 20 smaller ones. The Caspian Sea is on the large Eurasian plate.

By the late *Mesozoic epoch* (about 170 to 135 million years ago), the Eurasian plate had rotated clockwise, closing off the eastern part of the ancient Tethys Sea. The Caspian's basin became landlocked for good. In fact the present Caspian Sea, Black Sea, and Mediterranean Sea are all that is left of the ancient Tethys Sea.

ORIGINS: MIDDLE STAGES

During the early *Miocene* (close to 25 million years ago), mountain building became vigorous here. The land was squeezed, folded, and shoved south. The Alps were rising during the period 37 million to 23 million years ago, which overlaps with the early Miocene. This was the period in which the Caspian's rich oil deposits formed.

By the time of the later *Pliocene* to *Pleistocene* (5 to 2 million years ago), *sediments* were filling in the lowlands of Eurasia. By the time these sediments reached about eight miles thick and solidified into rock in their lower layers, the folding began again, caused mostly by the Arabian plate shoving against the Eurasian plate. As the land folded, some of it rose to make the area's mountains higher, and some of it fell lower. Quite low now, the Caspian's basin began to deepen further in the southern part of what is now the lake.

Moving the Earth's crust here as though it were cooling taffy, the mountain building stretched the area in between the mountain ranges. That land is now under the northern part of the Caspian Sea. In a way mountain building uses up more than its local share of the Earth's crust, tugging it up and thus thinning the swatch of crust in between. The Earth's crust under the Caspian averages only five to 9.3 miles (8 to 15 km) thick, compared to a world average of about 21.75 miles (35 km) for continental crust. Thinner sections of crust then subside, or slump, more readily.

Because of all this mountain building, plate colliding, and land slumping in its origins, the Caspian Sea is classified as a lake formed by tectonic activity. To place that in perspective, please see Origin of the Landform: Lakes, earlier in the book, which describes the different ways lakes form.

DESERT SURROUNDINGS

The lowering of the land and the rising of the mountains set the stage for the Caspian Sea's next major feature, its desert surroundings and highly related to that, its extreme salinity. (Its dryness can be seen in the color insert on page C-1.)

High mountains change weather, and the mountains in the Caspian Sea's part of the world began to do that immediately. They still do it today. Mountains cause the rain clouds that blow toward them to pile up on the side of the prevailing winds; the mountains and the warmer air they "exhale" are simply in the way of these clouds. The rain then falls on that side of the mountains or on the mountains themselves. Almost none is left to fall on or near the land on the far side of the mountains, here the Caspian basin. This phenomenon, called the *rainshadow* of the mountains, is a major force in creating the large deserts of the world, including the deserts of the Middle East. Even the Great Plains of the United States exists because that land lies in the rainshadow of the Rocky Mountains and so remains dry.

SALINE LAKES IN DRY ENVIRONMENTS

In North America, Europe, and areas of comparable latitude in the Southern Hemisphere, saline lakes are rather rare. Most of the lakes we know, from the Great Lakes to the pond in the local park, are not saltwater but freshwater. However, if one measures not the number of lakes but the volume of lake water, the total volume of water held by all the saline lakes on Earth would be almost as large as the volume held by all the freshwater ones. The Caspian Sea contributes a great deal to this equation.

Saline lakes are unusual in many ways. Salty water freezes, on average, at 28°F (−2.2°C), not 32°F (0°C) as freshwater does. So a lake's stratification (its layering based on heat exchange) is then different. Since salt water is heavier, it creates more water pressure, and that makes the lake colder at its deeper levels than would be the case in freshwater. Salty lakes generally have a fewer number of species inhabiting them than freshwater lakes do, but these saline lakes usually have more individuals within the species they do have. In the salty lakes the Sun's rays tend to penetrate more deeply; this is one of the many things about these lakes that is not well understood and will require attention from the geologists of the future.

Overall, saline lakes have not been as extensively studied as freshwater ones, since freshwater is essential to human survival. The Caspian, however, has received a lot of research attention from geologists because of its oil and gas reserves.

In a dry environment such as the one in this part of the world, the Caspian Sea waters evaporate readily, precipitating out the salt, and though the Volga River's incoming water has been significantly reduced by upstream dams, plenty of water remains in the Caspian Sea. Owens Lake, in California, once fed by the Owens River from the Sierra Nevada, has not been so lucky. Its water was diverted to benefit Los Angeles (whose land was once a desert) and Owens "Lake" has become a 110-square-mile (285-km²) lakebed as dry as dust, all year long. The dry land is so salty that no plant on Earth can grow there.

This salty soil is lifted by the winds, and the blowing dust is a major problem. The dust here is made of silt and sand laced with arsenic. It has become our country's largest single source of dust, airborne, inhaled by people, and dangerous to them. It creates air pollution alerts.

Engineers are channeling part of the Owens River back toward its "lake" by pipeline, even though this reduces the flow of water to Los Angeles. Owens Lake will appear again, shallow—but at least swallowing its own nasty dust. For a lake whose dust will remain toxic for a much longer time, please see the next chapter, on the Aral Sea.

Rainshadows are broad "shadows" indeed. (Chapter 5: Lake Titicaca also discusses them.) They have made the Caspian area a desert, which the heat of the area has helped hugely to maintain. Of course some water has fallen or flowed into the Caspian basin throughout history. Rivers do find their way here. Gradually, water filled the basin to form the lake.

RIVERS

The rivers flowing into the Caspian Sea from the south and east include the Kura, the Selfid-rud, the Atrek, and the Aras. They traverse a lot of desert and, throughout the long, hot summers, evaporation claims a great deal of their water.

The rivers from the north and west, including Samur, the Sulak, the Terek, the Ural, and the Volga, are wider to begin with and contribute much more water. They also drain much larger *watersheds* or drainage areas, and their watersheds include mountains, which contribute snowmelt. More northerly, these rivers do not always traverse hot desert. Without the northern rivers, along with some seabed springs, the Caspian would have dried up long ago. Rivers as a whole bring in 80 percent of the Caspian's water, groundwater springs, and seepage between 2 and 9 percent, and precipitation contributes only the small remaining portion.

The Volga River, 2,291 miles (3,687 km) long, is by far the major influence on the Caspian's water budget. It brings in more than three-fourths of the river water volume reaching the lake. The Volga creates a delta 124 miles (200 km) broad as it enters from the north. Though the

LIFE IN THE CASPIAN

Across the planet the largest number of species of living things live in true saltwater—the oceans. Second in popularity to this full saltwater habitat is the freshwater one. The fewest number of species occupy the in-between, brackish water of places like the Caspian Sea. Within this the very lowest number live in salinities of 5 to 7 percent. The Caspian's salinity averages from about 3 percent to about 8 percent, depending upon the area one is testing. So it has relatively few species. (To put this in perspective, note that the very freshest freshwater contains 64 pounds of salt per cubic foot ($1,027 kg/m^3$) of water, and the saltiest level in the oceans is 64.2 pounds per cubic foot ($1,028 kg/m^3$).

Most species that manage to live in saline lakes evolved first to live in freshwater and then adapted to places like the Caspian. Two of the adaptations are a relatively impermeable body surface (to keep salt from being absorbed and fresher fluids from being eliminated) and an ability to get rid of salt easily. Some birds look a little as though they are crying because they can get rid of salt through their eye ducts. Other creatures produce very salty urine. Excess salt remaining in the body is fatal to most creatures.

The Caspian is home to untold numbers of bacteria and algae (common across the planet), with each species here adapted to a narrow range of the broad spectrum of salinities within the lake. Also inhabiting it are crabs, crayfish, bivalves (animals with two parts of their shells hinged, such as a clam or oyster), mollusks, some sponges, and other invertebrates. These are available to be eaten by the larger creatures.

The very largest inhabitants are the sturgeon of the Caspian, giant fish who look primitive and are indeed ancient species. At about 200 million years old, the sturgeon is one of the oldest species on earth. Three of these ancient species are fished here extensively, the beluga sturgeon most of all. Its eggs are prized as an exceptional caviar, and the demand for them is very high.

Unfortunately, the beluga has been significantly overfished. Azerbaijan captures about 80 percent of the sturgeon in the world, right here in the Caspian Sea. The fish is also suffering from the pollution, which will surely not diminish as oil and gas resources are further exploited. The belugas are already contaminated with DDT, PCBs, and other organochlorine compounds. Their numbers have dropped dramatically.

Even if progress is being made to preserve the beluga's numbers, which is not clear, results would not be significant for a long time. It takes this fish many decades to reach the size that used to be common in the Caspian, its prehistoric army of fish.

Elburz Mountains on the Caspian Coast, Iran *(CORBIS)*

Volga's water has been diverted, dammed, and even poisoned by agricultural and industrial chemicals, it is still the lifeblood of the Caspian Sea.

Perhaps surprisingly, the water level of the Caspian is not now falling. In fact it is known for its swings up and down. Since 1978, for example, it has risen enough to flood some oil wells in spring and summer, adding to the "oiliness" of the lake's low quality water. (More oil seeps out from natural vents.)

SALINITY

Desert surroundings and changes in lake level do not automatically mean a salty lake, but the two are related. Most saline lakes on this planet are in desert areas, including the Great Salt Lake in Utah, subject of chapter 9. Water evaporates more in hot, dry climates, which leaves the natural salt behind. Changes in lake level can then leave these salt deposits exposed on shore.

The salts do not come from the desert sand or the ocean directly. They build up as salty air blows in from the ocean, as rocks, soils, and wind-borne dust release their natural salts, as soils erode, as rivers flow in, and as the evaporating water leaves behind its minerals. The rocks here at the Caspian also hold ancient salt deposits, dating back to when this area was part of the Tethys Sea, one of our planet's early oceans. North of the Caspian lies a huge area of salty deposits and rock like this. In fact it is part of one of the six-largest ancient "evaporitic basins" on the planet

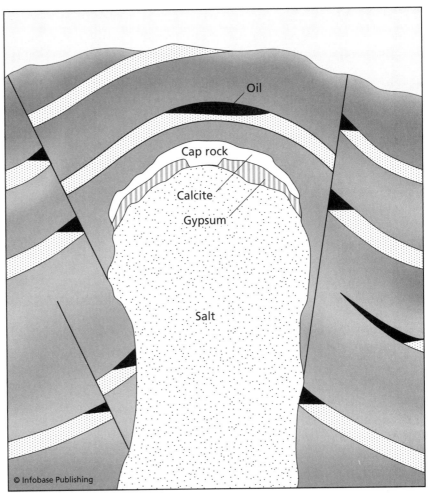

Salt domes like this lie just underground near the Caspian Sea, and the darkest areas show where oil is typically found.

(low, evaporated areas). The saltiness of the Caspian is also greatly enhanced as humans add both air and water pollutants, which contain salts.

And here there is less water to dilute all these additions, since the Caspian is in a dusty, desert environment, as can be seen in the color insert on page C-1. Salinity levels average high here, nearly 13 parts salt per thousand of water, with up to 200 parts per thousand as the maximum in certain areas of the Caspian Sea.

The salt of the Caspian is complex. It contains the common sodium of table salt, and also calcium, magnesium, potassium, bicarbonate, carbonate, sulfate, and chloride. Bromine, strontium, phosphate, and boron (not salts) also can be present. The balance among these chemicals is different in various areas of the lake, and microbes in the lake use and change its composition too.

SALT FEATURES

With all its salt, the Caspian has created some unusual geological salt features—and on a very large scale. One, called the Kara-Bogaz-Gol, is a natural evaporation area off the east shoreline. It is even lower in elevation than the Caspian Sea itself, about nine feet (2.7 m) lower. Here, throughout the year, the lake floods throughout the spring, then recedes through evaporation in the summer, leaving bare salt deposits. These are quite extensive. In one place the salt lies seven feet (2.1 m) thick, and covers an area of more than 1,000 square miles (2,590 km²).

Salt also is concealed onshore, underground, in the Caspian area. These features, called salt domes, are common all around the lake. Formed as heavy rock layers above, the salty layer presses down and forces the softer, more *plastic* salt to flow up and around harder rock (they resemble armies of hidden hills). This shape is why they are called domes. The underground domes can be up to 500 feet (152 m) high. Their tops are just below the surface of the ground, since desert soils are continually blowing in to cover them. Over time salt can flow to the surface where it typically washes away.

Because this kind of compression and flow is also what leads to the pooling of oil deposits, the salt domes can be used as a marker for places to drill. Salt domes are found along the Gulf Coast of the United States, too, where they are also associated with oil.

TECTONIC FEATURES

Other geologic features of the Caspian Sea include earthquakes, submerged volcanoes, mud volcanoes, and other signs of the tectonic forces acting here today. This is a restless area.

Earthquakes are a danger especially on the south and east sides of the Caspian Sea. A deadly one hit Bam, Iran, in late 2003, killing thousands. A bit farther south, Iran's capital, Tehran, could experience a major quake at any time. Periodically, Iranians discuss moving their capital, and all its 12 million residents, farther from this zone, but they have not done so.

Volcanic eruptions (volcanism) seem to have been going on in the Caspian Sea area for about 1.5 million years, with major periods of activity, in different parts of the Caspian area, at 1.2, 1.1, and 0.8 million years ago. What spews out of a volcano when it erupts is *magma* or hot flowing lava rock. Here, the magma forms as the crust under the Caucasus Mountains is heated until the rock flows. The crust crumples and collides underground because of the convergence of the Arabian and the Eurasian plates. Their smashing provides the energy.

Also here are mud "volcanoes." Associated with geological *faults* in areas rich in oil and natural gas resources, these are not truly volcanoes. Almost never hugely explosive, they are bubbling blobs of mud, clay, salty water, and methane gas pushing up through mud and shale rocks of the seafloor. They usually bring a bit of oil up with them—and sometimes a fish!

The tectonic activity that created the Caspian Sea's basin is still shaping the land here today. It will not end in the foreseeable future.

OIL AND NATURAL GAS

The geology of the Caspian makes it an area extremely rich in oil and natural gas resources. Coal and uranium are also mined here.

The Miocene (25 to 5 million years ago) was the most prolific period, worldwide, for the formation of these valuable fossil fuels. During the Miocene in the Caspian area, mountains were rising and *sediments* were filling in the low elevations alongside and between them. Sediments here reached eight miles (12.9 km) thick, significantly thicker than the typical few kilometers (or a couple of miles) of sediment found as the top layer of continental crust around the world.

These thick sediments, compressed by the immense weight of rock layers above them, and heated by the force of this pressure over millions of years, are what make oil. The gasoline we pump into our cars is called a "fossil fuel" because it is literally made of fossils—the dead plants, animals, and soils that compose the sediments—pressed so hard for so long that they have turned into a thick liquid slurry lying within small spaces in the rock. The process is a little like smashing a ripe peach with the heel of your hand—it will yield some peach juice along with the pulp.

The most lucrative area for oil and natural gas here is called the Caspian Depression. This huge, low desert wraps around the north and some of the east side of the present lake. There are many other areas of the Caspian that are also rich in oil. (Economic geologists study these resources.)

IN THE FIELD: LAKE LEVELS
AND CORE SAMPLING

Geologists are actively studying the Caspian Sea. Their major areas of interest include: the lake's water levels, its climate, salinity and other water chemistry, and its economic geology and environmental change. One of their research techniques will be described for each of these areas of study.

The water levels of the Caspian throughout its history reveal very large changes and seem to show cycles, the reasons for which are not yet well understood. Geopolitically, this area was long part of the Soviet Union, when most outside scientists were not allowed in to study it. That changed after the Union split apart in 1991. Geologists typically figure out earlier shorelines by analyzing the sediments near its present shore and underwater; fossils of fish indicate that the area was once underwater, for example.

The Caspian was probably at its most extensive about 1.2 million years ago, swollen with snowmelt from the glaciers of Europe. (The water entered via the Volga River.) And, in fact, it has had several very wide swings during five different phases of glaciation in the Pleistocene (2 million years ago to today), the period of glaciers on the planet. Glaciers never pushed as far south as the Middle East, but their meltwater made all the rivers wide and full.

To establish sea levels by examining sediments, geologists dig them up very carefully so as not to destroy or muddy the evidence. This is typically done by core sampling. (This technique is very important in geology and is also discussed in chapter 4: Lake Baikal, chapter 5: Lake Titicaca, chapter 6: Lake Vänern, and chapter 10: Great Slave Lake.) Using a long hollow metal tube and mechanical power (a kind of mining machine), the geologist team forces the tube down through the loose beach sand or underwater muck and farther down through a few feet up to a few hundred yards or more of solid rock. Many of those rock layers were once sediments, now compressed into layers of soil, solid rock, and the detritus of living things. The core is then pulled straight back up within its metal casing.

The next step is often to freeze-dry the core, hardening it to keep it together as the outer metal casing is removed. The core sample of rock is then cut into thin slices at points, which appear relevant to the geologists. These ancient layers are analyzed in various high-tech ways, using, for example, X-rays, *gas chromatography, mass spectrometry*, and other techniques. This is done back in the geology lab with the help of technicians.

Results are then compared by the geologist to the historical record—a measuring stick, in a sense—established by previous geological work. Direct measurements of the lake levels here go back about 100 years, only a start. There are other, very long-term benchmarks. One of these involves looking at the magnetic orientation of the magnetic rocks in the various core slices. (Not every rock is magnetic, of course, but a core sample will usually include some of these iron-rich rocks.) The Earth itself is a magnet because of its iron-rich *core*—and this "whole planet magnet" has changed its polarity, or north-south orientation, periodically throughout history. It has flipped, as though the whole Earth were a bar magnet that changed its ends from north to south and south to north. Every rock on the planet follows the lead of the Earth's core at the time that rock solidifies, and some rocks have enough magnetism that their north-south orientation can be measured. This technique can help establish the age of a core sample slice since the "flips" of the planet have been dated; many have occurred even over the past 70 million years, creating a useful yardstick. (For more on magnetic polarity shifts, please see chapter 4: Lake Baikal and chapter 5: Lake Titicaca.)

In addition to the magnetism, the basic mineral nature of the rock in the core samples is also investigated. It reveals much, such as when the lake was saltiest. This is visible as a layer where carbon-rich rock is more common than average—this chemical is precipitated out of water during evaporation, and evaporation is associated with higher salinity. Was a lagoon present here in certain periods, or was this area never underwater? Core sampling helps to figure this out also.

IN THE FIELD: LAKE LEVELS AND THEIR DATES

Using core sampling and other research methods, geologists have put together other information on the Caspian's water levels and looked for cycles or patterns in its changes. They have found that during the *Holocene* (from 10,000 years ago to today), also considered part of the Pleistocene, the lake has gone up and down 60 feet (18 m). Between 1929 and 1995, lake levels oscillated 20 feet (6 m) alone, which included a dramatic lowering during the 1930s. The Caspian is currently considered high. Cycles of both 62.5 and 38.46 years in its rises and falls have been suggested but not completely accepted. And some geologists have predicted that the lake will increase in size during this century. Much remains to be learned here, and this geological research certainly has implications for where the area's people should live, where they should explore for oil, and other such decisions.

The causes for the changes in Caspian water level remain to be figured out also. Some geologists think Northern Hemisphere climate change is key. Others point to changes on the Sun (in its sunspot, or major storm, activity) as affecting world climate in complicated ways not well understood. Others focus on tectonic changes, earth movements that change the shape of the lake's basin. And there are additional theories, too.

As more is learned about the Caspian's changes in water level, that will, in turn, enhance our understanding even of the glaciers and glacial melt in the Soviet Arctic in Pleistocene times (about 2 million years ago to current times), since the glacial meltwater caused lake levels to rise. In fact, *paleogeology*, the use of present studies to tell us about the distant past, is an interest of many geologists. This kind of research is quite productive at the Caspian Sea.

IN THE FIELD: CLIMATE, SALINITY, AND OTHER WATER CHEMISTRY

Among the techniques used by paleogeologists is the analysis of pollen spores. Powerful special microscopes can identify and analyze the tiny tree and plant pollen spores found in the core samples. Cooler weather and warmer weather are better for different groups of plants, which then release more pollen during their heydays. One pollen study, which looked at 116 different species of pollen spores, suggested that summers were significantly cooler at the Caspian Sea about 6,000 years ago than they are today. Geologists can rely on comparing the ancient pollen to known pollens from various plants today since a plant's pollen does not change much.

Climate changes throughout history at the Caspian Sea can also be glimpsed at by looking at the fossils of the sea creatures and plant detritus found in the core samples. Warmer or cooler periods can cause species to be eliminated entirely—their fossils may be present in one layer and absent in another, suggesting a change in climate.

The salinity of the Caspian, probably its most salient feature, has received a great deal of research attention also. Since the lake includes a variety of salts, and since the rivers bring in fresher water, salinity varies throughout the lake. In one area alone it ranges from 3.2 percent to 7.4 percent. The salinity can help to concentrate metal pollutants in places where a major river flows in. And it is also being studied to investigate the economics of desalination, or turning salty water into freshwater, for human or at least industrial purposes. This is now very expensive, given our present technology.

Many other aspects of the lake's water chemistry are under study. Among them are its levels of trace uranium and the change in position of the Volga River's delta. Large-scale movements of water within the lake, which would mix its chemistry significantly, are apparently rare. The two deepest areas exchange only 7 percent of their water per year. Another subject studied, with implications for drilling, is mud circulation. Techniques used here include aerial photography and remote sensing to map large-scale vegetation features.

IN THE FIELD: ECONOMIC GEOLOGY

Economic geology is a very important area of research in the Caspian area, though fewer of its results are found in the regular scientific journals than other areas of research. Many economic geologists work for big oil and gas drilling and processing companies, which want to keep the research private in order to use it in their business. Corporate investments in the Caspian have also only been possible since the Soviet Union broke up in 1991, but they are fast and extensive now. The exploitation of salt resources here, active for well over 100 years, has become large-scale since the 1970s; though part of economic geology, it has not been a subject of so much secrecy.

Among the things discovered in the Caspian area is that there are at least six major underwater areas rich in oil and gas (in addition to the areas on land); the latest new area of 100 promising sections was discovered just in late 2004. There may also be large pockets of natural gas trapped in thick layers of rock below the Caspian Sea. Other researchers have looked at what might be the cheapest, but not necessarily the shortest, route for pipelines to move the area's immense oil and gas resources to markets around the world.

Economic geology techniques include directing *seismic* waves down through the water or ground. Geologists can monitor how these waves may be slowed, or sped up, or bent, depending upon whether they are passing through oil or nonoil sands or sediments. (For more on seismic techniques, please see chapter 8: Crater Lake.)

Geological research in the Caspian also relates to environmental changes connected to oil exploitation. The Caspian has become a quite polluted place. Oil and oil by-products leak into the lake, introducing contaminants such as PAHs (polycyclic aromatic hydrocarbons). Methane also pollutes the lake, as a result of natural gas and coal exploitation. The fossil fuel industries also emit carbon, sulfur, and nitrogen oxides. Radiation levels here are boosted by oil and uranium mining. In addition, mercury and metal concentrations in the lake are too high, probably also the result of mining operations. There is tremendous opportunity for geologists to help with problems like these, here and elsewhere.

The Caspian Sea is an immense lake. The saltiest lake in the world, partially surrounded by desert, its elevation is low and climate hot. The area is rich in resources from salt to oil and gas, though these industries as well as others are contributing to its pollution.

✧ 2 ✧✧✧✧✧✧✧✧✧✧✧✧✧✧✧✧✧✧✧✧✧✧✧

Aral Sea

Western Asia

If the Caspian Sea (the subject of chapter 1) sounds like an oddly un-attractive and environmentally degraded place, the Aral Sea could announce itself as actually horrifying. Movie producers without concern for personal health could shoot a horror flick here. Readers may choose to place this lake on a long list of sites to visit around the world—in last place.

After the preliminaries the degradation of the Aral Sea will be described. But do note: the rest of the lakes in this book are all wonderful to encounter.

The Aral Sea, bordered by Kazakhstan and Uzbekistan, lies north of the Caspian Sea in central Asia and east of the Ural Mountains (considered the dividing line between Europe and Asia). Unlike the Caspian, it has neither significant oil and gas resources, nor big cities nearby. Like the Caspian, it is called a "sea" because of its size, though it is, too, a lake, unconnected to any ocean.

The Aral lies in an arid region of grassland steppes and desert plateaus, its environs a lot more like the Middle East than Europe. To its north and northwest the Aral's area is mountains and grasslands. A low salty area lies to its east and southeast, and a much larger lower one stretches far to its north. A true desert called the Peski Bol'shiye Barsuki extends east and west of the Aral. The lake was once fed by two vigorous rivers, the Syr Darya and the Amu Darya, though they are now much diminished in flow. It has three islands, Lazerew Oroli, Ostrov Barsakel'mes, and Vozrozhdeniye; the latter, to which we shall return later, is commonly called Renaissance Island or Rebirth Island but is a dangerous place.

FORMATION

The formation of the Aral Sea occurred because of *tectonic forces*, the large-scale movements of vast rocky *plates* that alter the position of the Earth's landmasses over millions, even billions, of years. (These forces

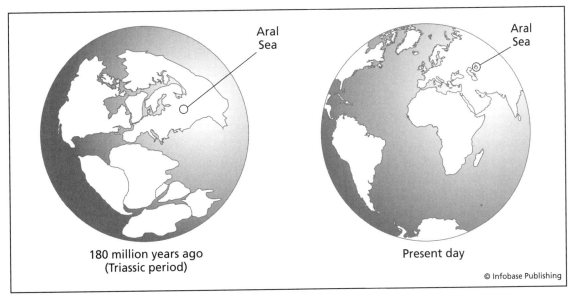

180 million years ago
(Triassic period)

Present day

© Infobase Publishing

This schematic of the continents' locations 180 million years ago shows that the Aral Sea was once nearer to the ocean's edge.

are commonly called *plate tectonics.*) Very early in the *Paleozoic epoch* (500 to 235 million years ago), the continents were joined closely together; but in what would become this part of the world, the land began to split and fold. A north-south strip gradually rose to become the Ural Mountains, this uplift zone extending from just north of the Aral and Caspian Seas all the way to the Arctic. To the east and south of this uplifted land lay part of an ancient ocean called the Tethys Sea. Part of this salty sea lay over the land that is now the Aral.

By the end of the Paleozoic, in a time period within it called the *Permian* (270 to 235 million years ago), the Aral's general area became part of a huge "evaporitic basin." The combination of salt deposits from the nearby Tethys Sea, the relatively low elevation, and the high temperatures created a place where water evaporated to leave this low area of salty soil. Two vast areas north of the Aral and Caspian are known as one of the three largest such evaporitic basins on the planet.

During the next epoch, the *Mesozoic* (235 to 70 million years ago), the continents finished this period of splitting and landmasses reached close to their present positions. The basin that would become the Aral Sea became hot and desertlike, even though the Ural Mountains beyond and two rivers (now called the Syr and the Amu) flow toward it.

Last, during the *Cenozoic epoch* (70 million years ago to the present), the old Tethys Sea area became completely reconfigured as more mountains were built. The *tectonic plates* that carry what is now Africa and

India collided with the Eurasian plate. The masses of rock that uplifted, then piled up, became the Alps, the Himalayas, and other ranges such as the Caucasus. The Urals were also reshaped. The Indian Ocean and the Mediterranean took their present positions far from the Aral Sea area, and the Tethys Sea vanished.

PRESENT FORM

Between these mountain ranges lower areas began to fill with runoff water from the mountains. One of these lower areas is now the Aral Sea. It has been here for about 2 million years.

This part of the world has remained *tectonically active*, though the lands south of the Caspian Sea are much more so than the Aral Sea's environs. In our present era the Aral has been shaped more by human action than by tectonic forces.

The Aral Sea was once the largest freshwater lake in the world. As recently as 1960, it was rich in fish and fresh enough to drink. Then this scenario changed. The lake became one of the world's worst environmental disasters, one that is still unfolding today.

DRASTIC CHANGES BEGIN

Since 1960 the Aral Sea has shrunk 70 percent in water volume and split in two. By the 1990s it had shriveled to half its original extent. The lake's level fell by 52.5 feet (16 m), and its waters became three times as salty. Its shoreline receded 30 miles (48.25 km) in some places and up to 60 miles (96.5 km) in others, stranding former fishing villages in a new desert of toxic sand. Up to 85 percent of its cropland can now no longer be farmed. The Aral's rivers today bring in a dribble of pollution where once they supplied ample clean water.

The land in between the northern and southern parts of the Aral (once an underwater ridge) is also contaminated with salt and agricultural chemicals. One of the lake's islands, Rebirth Island, features an anthrax factory from the mid-20th century. This chemical, used as a weapon so toxic that less than a teaspoon can kill a city, still contaminates the soil there.

The slow, steady death of the Aral Sea continues today, damaging the health of the population around it, an area most broadly defined as 35 million people. Its degradation affects not only Kazakhstan and Uzbekistan but also Kyrgyzstan, Tajikistan, and Turkmenistan, all in its drainage basin.

There is, however, one bright spot. Because of a new dam and water diversions, the small, northern section of the former Aral (about one-seventh of the whole lake's now shrunken size) that has been long cut off from the large main southern section, is actually deepening. Levels have gone from fewer than 98 feet (30 m) to 125 feet (38 m). Though lake levels need to be 138 feet (42 m) to make fishing sustainable, some of the

"ANTHRAX ISLAND"

This Aral Sea island, whose name "Vozrozhdeniye" is translated as Renaissance Island or Rebirth Island, is the ultimate unwise destination for a tourist visit—even within the heavily polluted environs of this lake. Biological weapons were made here, and the mess has still not been completely cleaned up.

During the cold war of the 1950s through the 1980s, when the United States and other Western countries vied with the Soviet Union and other communist countries for power and control of the loyalties of the rest of the world, this island was part of that strife. It became home to research on anthrax, a deadly microbe that can be used to make weapons of mass destruction. The laboratory on the island also investigated the organisms that create other deadly conditions. None of these dangerous organisms is visible to the naked eye, making the island hard to clean even if there were enough money and commitment to do so.

After the Soviet Union disbanded in 1991, the facility here in the Aral Sea was shut down, and most of the "killer germs" were indeed deliberately exterminated. Anthrax, however, is particularly hard to dispose of—it lives easily in soil, spreading there to contaminate large stretches of land.

This island was never properly guarded, and now, with the shrinkage of the Aral Sea, people can actually walk out to it, as can be glimpsed in the color insert. Looters are a problem, and now so are small burrowing animals—soil that is contaminated could easily be walked right back to the mainland on their shoes and feet.

Not until 2001 was a clean-up agreement signed. The United States is paying Uzbekistan to decontaminate "Anthrax Island." Unfortunately, this has not yet been entirely accomplished.

After the events of September 11, 2001, a new visit was made here by United States officials. The goal was to see if any contaminants might be available to terrorists. Journalists who have inquired and visited since have not seen any real change, however.

fishermen, are returning. The main section of the Aral, however, is still likely to disappear.

REASONS FOR SHRINKAGE

In this part of the world precipitation is low, summer temperatures regularly climb to 120°F (48.8°C), and lake water evaporation is quick and common. So a lake needs to be fed by ample river water from more distant places, where rainfall is more abundant, and mountain rivers need to provide snowmelt. Two things have happened here to disrupt this system: Natural rainfall has been reduced, and the river system has gone completely awry. New islands also appear, as can be seen in the color insert on page C-1.

In the days of the Soviet Union (1917–91), a vast country that included all of the countries around the Aral Sea, the powerful central government decided to divert the Aral's two rivers. Their goal, which was largely met, was to use the river water as irrigation, allowing this area to grow vast tracts of cotton even though it is a desert or near-desert zone. An agricultural operation like this typically uses even more water per acre than a comparably sized city. The rivers were channeled away from their

In this aerial image one can see the shrinkage of the Aral as of its stage in 1985. *(NASA/CORBIS)*

courses and sent right through the cotton fields. Not only is cotton an especially "thirsty" crop—it needs water by gulps in order to grow—but also the irrigation ditches built to direct the water were not lined. A great deal of the water simply soaked into the ground without even reaching the cotton plants.

Agricultural chemicals, such as pesticides and fertilizers for increasing the cotton crop yields, were also added, and in excessive amounts. Large volumes of these pollutants, along with eroding salty soil, reached the Aral Sea in the vastly diminished volume of freshwater carried by the rivers. The two main rivers, the Syr and the Amu, once brought more than 24 cubic miles (100 km³) of water per year into the Aral. Now both rivers are narrower than 10 feet (3 m) wide. This recipe for a lake disaster, played out over decades, caused the Aral Sea to begin vanishing.

THE OCEANS OF THE WORLD AND THEIR SALT

Reading about the highly saline Caspian Sea and the increasingly salty Aral Sea, curious readers may wonder where the salt originally came from. The two lowland seas were once either under or very near the ancient Tethys Sea, an early ocean, which contributed quite a bit of saltiness to what is now the land here. But then where does an ocean get its salt?

One has to go back to the infancy of this planet to find the origin of the salt. The just-born Earth began about 4.6 billion years ago, a blob of hot rocky material, condensed from dust and pebbles in the solar nebula after the formation of the Sun. The rock quickly began to cool and one very common kind of rock, called "hydrous silicate minerals," sweated out its hydrogen and oxygen (its H_2O, water).

This water gradually rose up from all the interior rocks of the new Earth, dissolving other minerals along the way. The solution, already salty, collected on the surface in the slightly lower areas. Some of the water was also drawn up into the atmosphere, which was still hot, then later came down as rain when the air cooled. The highly soluble sodium and other salts remained in the water now deepening on the surface. So all the salty oceans of the world came from the first rocks.

EFFECTS OF THE SHRINKAGE

The effect of the lake's changes on the fish alone has been dramatic. Of the Aral Sea's major fish species, 20 out of 25 have died out completely. And, out of 178 species of animal in the area, only 38 species survive.

The 5 million people who live close enough to need the Aral for their livelihood and for drinking water do not have many ways to make a living in a part of the world so inhospitable to agriculture. They used to fish, but the fishing villages now find very few fish to catch, and what fish they do find are much farther away. To reach them, the people have to travel dozens of miles across polluted sand dunes instead of walking down the street as they once did.

It is estimated that 60,000 people have become unemployed as a result of this Aral Sea disaster. Some of them have moved upstream on the rivers and are proceeding to stress the water supply even more from there.

Projections are that, unless massively expensive improvements are made, the Aral Sea could completely disappear by about 2010.

HARD TO FIX

To see why the Aral Sea's future is so uncertain, one has to look at the geopolitics here, the politics heavily influenced by geography and geology. The countries in this area, once controlled by the central decisions of the old Soviet Union, are now fighting over the water, truly their lifeblood in such a dry section of the world. Kazakhstan, one of the two countries with Aral Sea shoreline, should be more prosperous than it is since its oil and gas resources are so vast. Yet it is mired in rural poverty, urban governmental corruption, and the stress of depending upon the neighboring countries of Tajikistan and Kyrgyzstan for freshwater from rivers that pass through those countries first. This is a recipe for significant conflict.

Uzbekistan, the other Aral Sea shoreline country, has an economy still far too dependent on its cotton crop, and, to a lesser extent, on rice (another crop that requires huge amounts of water). Its much smaller acreage of apricots and watermelons, also irrigation dependent, have mostly vanished for lack of water. The farmers are regularly moving upstream where the river water and land are less contaminated, but that creates more agricultural pollution there. Uzbekistan, a poorer country than Kazakhstan, also accuses Tajikistan of polluting the water farther upstream and argues with Kyrgyzstan over how much of the river water it is consuming.

To make matters even worse, Turkmenistan is building a large reservoir, a lake of about 770 square miles (2,000 km²) for its own "water security." Another reservoir lies at the Kazakhstan-Uzbekistan border, and the former country is resented by the others because it controls much of the Syr River flow.

This situation, called a "water war," is compounded here by the poverty of the countries involved. But all dry areas of the world, including Arizona, New Mexico, and Southern California, are in strife with their neighbors over water, too. This is a world of 6 billion people now, and counting, all requiring drinking water and, in dry areas, yet more water to grow food. The United Nations estimates that about 460 million people around the world are already affected by "water stress" and that this number could increase tenfold by the year 2025 if water consumption, especially in agriculture, is not reduced.

SALINITY

As has been mentioned, vast tracts of land north of the Aral Sea are an old evaporitic basin where salty soils and sands were formed in ancient times from the evaporation of nearby seawater and other forces. The Aral Sea is close to the edge of this very large region. And its own underlying land was also salty to some degree when the lake formed originally, because of the proximity of the ancient ocean, the Tethys Sea.

But unlike the Caspian Sea, which has long been intensely saline, the Aral Sea was once only slightly brackish, testing at about nine ounces of salt per gallon (70 g/l of salt) and people drank it. Now, it is mostly undrinkable (depending upon the location within the lake). And its water is verging on the drastic level of 18.7 ounces of salt per gallon (140 g/l of salt), which would be saltier than the ocean itself. Already, some 2.5 to 4 million people cannot safely drink the Aral's water—or even nearby groundwater, since it is polluted with salt and other chemicals. The Aral Sea's water now tests as three times as salty as the United Nations standard for safe drinking water. By 2000 some 85 percent of the adjacent land had even become too salty for agriculture. Salty water and soil do yet more damage. They create dangerous dust.

DUST

The direct effect on people's health of the geological disaster that is the Aral Sea is by far its worst result. Just as no one can safely drink salty and pesticide-laden water, no one can safely breathe air that includes salty and pesticide-laden sand and soil particles. When a lake like this shrinks, that is the kind of air pollution that results. Unpaved roads and overgrazed farm fields add even more fine dust to the air.

The shriveled shoreland that once was under the Aral Sea features large white *salt pans*, and some of the surface salt is swept up into the air. These flat areas look like the floor of Death Valley, California, and stretch so far here that, from an airplane, they are said to look like snow. Other areas, primarily dust, look a smudgy brown, as can be seen in the color insert on page C-2.

All this toxic dust becomes regularly airborne, and the desert winds and low levels of precipitation here make the problem even worse. It is estimated that about 43 million tons of dust a year clog the air around the Aral Sea, the highest volume anywhere on the planet.

About five times a year, dust storms rage so intensely that people must remain inside their homes for days at a time. There the air is a bit clearer. When they emerge, it is to shovel the toxic dust off the fields, outside the front door, and anywhere else they have the strength to do so. The inhaled dust has been found to contain particles of pesticides, fertilizers, cadmium, and other heavy metals not fit for human lungs.

HEALTH EFFECTS

Health is very poor around the Aral Sea. Asthma, childhood pneumonia, diarrhea, kidney disease, esophageal cancer, along with anemia and tuberculosis at the highest rates in the world, all are well above expected levels in both children and adults in the Aral Sea area. Infant mortality is high, as is emotional stress.

One researcher set up dust traps, fitted a pump to pull air across a filter to imitate a person's lungs drawing breath, and discovered the intake of dust to be four to five times greater than the United States Environmental Protection Agency guidelines for the dusty season in this country. The situation is the worst on the south side of the Aral Sea.

More than 100,000 people have already left the Aral area for good, and they tend to be the healthier ones who feel able to start a new life elsewhere. Though poverty contributes to the disease load, its origin is the air. And that air is a direct result of the lake's shrinkage.

WHAT CAN BE DONE

Though the Aral Sea began shrinking in 1960, the tragedy was gradual. And the Soviet Union's government rarely allowed any outside observers anywhere within its borders. It took until 1986–87 for the situation here to be recognized at all, and it was not well known until a few years after that. International and local efforts to begin help date back just to 1990. The countries that surround the Aral are now, and have always been, too poor to pay for the major improvements they need.

Among the key actions suggested have been: lining the irrigation ditches to ensure that the channeled river water at least reaches the crops, installing better drinking water treatment and medical care for the people, paving the roads and treating the industrial wastes to cut down on the dust, and switching agricultural production from cotton and rice to wheat and maize (which require less water). Population growth should also receive immediate attention, since it is projected to rise by about one-third over the next 25 years.

Many studies have been done on the Aral Sea and its environs. An old saying apparently popular here goes like this: "If everyone who came to study our problem had brought a bucket of water, the Aral Sea would be full again."

Ideas have come and gone; many international groups have simply given up for lack of money, and at least one bizarre solution has been abandoned. That was to build a new river channel to direct Arctic Ocean water down to here. (This would just substitute a new northern problem for this one.) Few people, if any, seem to think this lake can ever refill to its 1960 size.

One group still working hard in the Aral Sea area is Doctors Without Borders, physicians from around the world (especially Western countries) who do studies, equip laboratories, help raise funds for local medical supplies, and train local health care workers. They collect and maintain statistics on the human geotragedy at the Aral.

Many other researchers have come up with plans to raise money for improvements. Some of them employ taxation: taxing water use, salt discharges, and wasteful irrigation practices, and taxing even the increase in local profits if the international community pays for new industrial facilities and other improvements. Still others recommend that Aral Sea countries trade water for electricity among themselves. This would avoid the building of reservoirs by all the various competing countries (to make electricity, water must usually be dammed up to create enough force to push it through a turbine). Problems in cooperation among the countries and in funding, however, remain. It is not clear what will happen here.

IN THE FIELD: SATELLITE IMAGERY

Earth scientists are among the researchers who have found the basic, important information needed on the Aral Sea. One technique they have

THE BLACK SEA AND THE ORIGIN OF THE CARP

This immense body of water, far larger than the Aral Sea and larger even than the Caspian Sea, is not, however, a lake. It is connected to the Mediterranean Sea through the Straits of Bosporus (once an old river valley) at the city of Istanbul, Turkey.

The Black Sea is also bordered by Georgia, Russia, Ukraine, Romania, and Bulgaria and is considered to be part Europe and part Middle East. Its major contributing rivers are the Dnieper, the Danube, and the Don, and its major mountain range the Caucasus on its east coast. Along the south coast grows the world's biggest crop of hazelnuts.

The wild carp, ancestor of all the species of carp now found in the freshwater lakes and rivers of the world, originated as a species in the Black Sea, Caspian Sea, and Aral Sea. The fish spread, evolving all the way, to China, Germany, and Siberia. After that, humans imported it to extend its range elsewhere. It is now common in the United States and in many other places around the world.

Some people love this fish. The Japanese have bred a species called the colored carp and nicknamed it the "swimming flower." Other people consider it unpleasant.

used is satellite imagery. Satellite photos and heat sensors can establish both the water levels and water temperatures of the Aral and how they are changing. Among the findings is that, as the lake has shrunk, summer in the area has become hotter and winter colder, by several degrees. Using a different satellite, one that looks for data on the magnetism of areas it passes over, other geologists have seen that the geologic fault under the Ural Mountains may extend south to the middle of the Aral Sea. This would create the potential for earthquakes in certain areas and affect what should be built there. Another team has used soil samples to discover where the worst of the dust storms originate.

The Aral Sea is a living warning of what can happen when a lake's water quality issues are ignored. Low in elevation, salty, hot, unhealthy, and an object of strife among the countries around it, this lake is shrinking and may well disappear entirely.

Lake Superior

North America

This is the largest freshwater lake in the world, an expanse of blue that looks almost as wide as the sky itself. Lake Superior holds about 10 percent of the planet's entire supply of surface freshwater—an estimated 2,860 cubic miles (11,921 km³) of it, enough to equal the water of the other three Great Lakes, plus three Lake Eries, combined. It stretches over nearly 32,000 square miles (82,880 km²). A ship traversing this lake east to west, its longest dimension, travels 376 miles (605 km) from Duluth, Minnesota (the westernmost point of all the Great Lakes), to Sault Ste. Marie, the city astride the United States–Canada border, where Lake Superior meets Lake Huron at its easternmost point. Its expanse from north to south is 160 miles (258 km) at the widest point. The lake has 1,026 miles (1,651 km) of shoreline and is the highest of the Great Lakes in elevation, at 602 feet (183.5 m) above sea level.

Bordered by Minnesota, the Canadian province of Ontario, Michigan, and Wisconsin, Lake Superior is the most northerly of the Great Lakes. Water temperatures average 39 to 40°F (4°C) year round. This is cold enough to kill an unprotected swimmer in about 20 minutes, even in summertime (unless it is possible to make it back to a warmer, shallow cove by the shore).

In the fall, when the air temperature around Lake Superior drops, the lake gradually loses its "heat." This means it can release enough heat in one day to equal all the energy consumed in the United States in one year.

Winter means ice. Lake Superior freezes over enough of its surface to stop major ship travel, but there are almost always some open areas, called polynas, where currents stir the water enough to keep ice from forming. In 1979, an unusually cold year, its entire surface froze over, for a few hours.

By early spring ice caves appear along its North Shore. Created by slushy water surges and surf that pile up and refreeze, some of these caves can seat a dozen people inside on ice block "chairs." Many of these seasonal caves are large enough for a brief two-person picnic, refrigeration no extra charge.

In summer, when Lake Superior can warm up to 45°F (7°C), it still serves as a kind of "air conditioner" for people living close to its shores. In Duluth, for example, almost no one owns an ordinary air conditioner, though along the south shore, and occasionally on the north, people do wade into Lake Superior on hot days to cool off.

DEPTH AND TIDES

This lake plunges to 1,330 feet (405 m) deep. Because of this depth, it churns up violent storms, especially in November before it freezes, and is known as the "graveyard of ships." The *Edmund Fitzgerald*, subject of folk songs and other lore, is the most famous example. But hundreds of other large ore ships lie on its bottom, everything preserved in cold storage. Powerful underwater currents sweep the sand off some wrecks every year and bury others anew. Except in those places and times, the lake is extremely clear. You can see 65 to 75 feet (20 to 23 m) down much of the time.

Scuba divers, outfitted in tightly fitting gear for warmth, visit some of the underwater wrecks in summertime, as well as the underwater sea caves. They avoid the temporary "benthic storms" that can roil the water even on the bottom, like submerged thunderstorms. Kayakers go out in summer, too, usually remaining close to the shoreline or among island archipelagoes. A few people have kayaked all around the lake, braving winds that could smash them quickly into the boulders on the shore.

Lake Superior does have a tide, since tides are created by the Moon's gravity tugging on the Earth's bodies of water. But, since this lake is "small"—compared to an ocean—the largest difference between low tide and high tide is less than an inch, unnoticed.

More dramatic are the "seiches," giant-scale sloshes of water. A seiche can make the lake suddenly up to 12 inches (30.5 cm) deeper across vast areas than it was just an hour before. These water movements are created as though the lake were a coffee cup tilting back and forth. The movement begins in storms far away. Storms arrive with low barometric pressure, and this means that the atmosphere is pressing down less hard on the lake where the storm is than the atmosphere would ordinarily do. With less pressure pressing down, the lake level rises in that area. If the storm is large and situated over one end of the lake, and the water there rises, that lowers the water elsewhere on the lake and the sloshing begins. Then it sloshes back making the water much deeper. The effect arrives invisibly (the storm is at the other end of the lake) and vanishes invisibly. A seiche lasts anywhere from several hours up to 24 hours. (In Lake Michigan, where swimming is common, swimmers find them fun.)

Split Rock lighthouse sits high on a headland of Lake Superior's North Shore. *(www.shutterstock.com)*

SLATE ISLANDS

In northern Lake Superior the Slate Islands lie about 6.2 miles (10 km) off the Canadian North Shore. This archipelago was created by the impact of a giant meteorite, about 450 million years ago. No one was near because people did not yet exist. Neither did any of the land animals here today. Not even the lake itself was here.

This ancient disaster left a complex crater, now surrounded and partly submerged by Lake Superior's waters. Its edges lie about 1.2 miles (2 km) from the center point. The largest of the Slate Islands is about 4.3 miles (7 km) in diameter. Though this impact site is certainly large, it was once larger, probably 18 to 20 miles (30 to 32 km) across. Erosion, from wave action during storms, has gradually worn away at the island's rock mass.

Scientists know that a meteorite smashed here since its force shocked and then heated the rock already there, creating some new rocks with glassy intrusions and shattered fragments within them. These rocks are called *breccias* and *tektites*. It also exposed some ancient rock, about 3 billion years old, that would otherwise have remained buried.

Today the Slate Islands are home to hundreds of woodland caribou, safe here from the wolves. Though they are wild animals, they have become so unafraid of humans over so many generations, that they will sometimes eat a carrot out of a person's hand.

In addition to woodland caribou, the North Shore of Lake Superior is rich in other wildlife such as wolves, black bears, coyotes, moose, beaver, deer, muskrats, bobcats, some lynx, skunks, fishers, fox, raccoons, squirrels, and chipmunks. Woodland creatures are able to hide easily and tend to be shy of people. One could hike all 400 miles (644 km) of the beautiful trails on the North Shore section of the lake in Minnesota and see only a few deer, perhaps a moose, and, of course, the squirrels and chipmunks. This is not a dangerous place unless you try to go swimming in the cold water.

There are also many birds here. In fact the North Shore is one of the major "bird factories" of the country. More than 140 different species nest in Lake Superior's woods. A springtime trip with binoculars can mean seeing 60 species in a day.

WATERSHED

Lake Superior is fed by rivers much too numerous to mention, and they drain massive amounts of rain and snowmelt into the lake, adding to the large volume of precipitation that falls on it directly. Especially on the North Shore, many of the rivers originate in wild peat lands and traverse only forested wilderness on their way to the lake, tumbling down waterfalls and gradually carving gorges. Though the forest was once logged heavily here (and some logging continues), there are still areas of boreal forest (high northern woods, composed of mostly evergreens common in Canada) on the North Shore. The area is home to cliffs, evergreens, and hardwoods, all along the North Shore, as can be seen in the color insert on page C-2.

The lake's *watershed* covers 525,000 square miles (1,359,743 km²). Since Superior lies in a temperate area of the world, and north within that zone, temperatures are not often hot. So evaporation out of the lake is less than new water into the lake. Lake Superior feeds the Atlantic Ocean some of its water through Lakes Huron, Erie, and Ontario, then via the St. Lawrence Seaway to the sea.

The timber industry, copper-nickel-iron mining and processing, paper production, fishing, and tourism characterize the North Shore. The South Shore has fertile soil, logging, fishing, and tourism. It no longer has copper mining. With only two smallish cities on its shores, Duluth, Minnesota, and Thunder Bay, Canada, as well as a scattering of small towns, the Lake Superior area is low in population. This helps to keep the lake clear and fresh, and its cold temperatures mean it holds plenty of dissolved oxygen. Very, very little algae and few other water plants live in it.

ORIGIN

The land that now forms Lake Superior's basin and environs, particularly on the Canadian North Shore stretch, is about as ancient as anything on Earth. It dates back to within the *Precambrian epoch* and is at least 2.7 to 2.6 billion years old. The first crustal *plates* on the planet formed only about 3.6 billion years ago (with solid rock only about 400 million years older than that). So this expanse of land is nearly as old as any that has been found, or probably will ever be.

The lake lies within the largest single area of this Precambrian rock on the Earth, called the Canadian Shield. Shields, and *cratons* are the oldest, most geologically stable, central sections of the Earth's continents. These areas are distinguished from the *mobile belts*, the active earthquake and volcanic zones at the continental edges.

AFTER THE LAND FORMED

The land here now was not always here. *Plate tectonics* has reworked and remodeled the planet a great deal (and continues to do so). About 2.7 billion years ago plate collisions and early volcanoes made mountains in the Lake Superior area, especially during the period 2.2 to 1.9 billion years ago. Leftover from this period are a few ancient granite cliffs on the North Shore's hiking trails and a very few granite rocks on its beaches. These mountains have all worn down. In fact the Canadian Shield has been called a bunch of mountain stumps.

Though there are usually layers of rock and soil over them now, lands under and near Lake Superior hold interesting fossils. Fossils of some of the earliest forms of life on the planet—algae and bacteria—can be found in what is now the North Shore.

Events that happened so long ago are obviously quite difficult to reconstruct. Was this land once part of a very ancient supercontinent, older than *Pangaea?* Why do the Baltic and Siberian Shields look similar

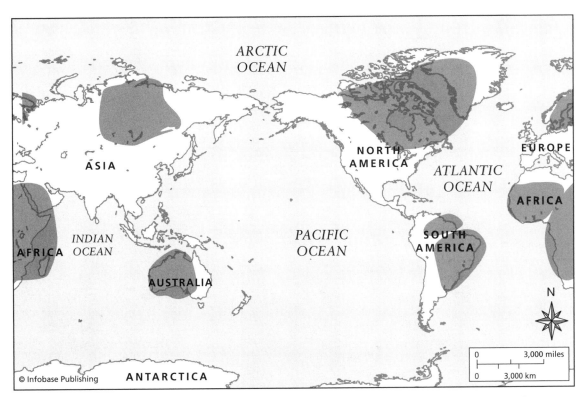

The dark areas of the continent are the shields, the oldest and most stable rock masses on the planet today.

to the Canadian Shield here? Were they once joined? How might the breakup of such a vast area relate to climate change in ancient times? Looking back 2.7 to 1.9 billion years ago is extremely difficult since the rock layers have been tilted, mixed, covered, eroded, and shoved around. There is a lot of interesting geology left to investigate in the Lake Superior region.

A FAILED OCEAN

What happened next in the Lake Superior region is a bit more clear. The land split apart. This split ran in a jagged line from Ontario to northeastern Minnesota to Kansas, and, in a lesser branch, down to Ohio. The length of this crack in the Earth's crust was more than 1,243 miles (2,000 km).

The event, called the Mid-Continent Rift of North America, happened from about 1.1 billion years ago to about 1 billion years ago, occurring over about 100,000 years. If this major *tectonic* rifting had continued, there would be an ocean today, right down the middle of the United States. What is now Gulf of Mexico water would have flowed

This schematic of the Mid-Continent Rift System of 1.1 billion years ago shows that Lake Superior was once part of this "failed ocean." The rift filled with lava.

right in. Basalt rock—the kind that forms the ocean crust today and that belches out as lava—is found all over the Lake Superior region.

This giant Mid-Continent Rift is no longer visible. Over the period of its formation, *magma* was also swelling up and spewing out of the rift even as it widened. By the time nearly 100,000 cubic miles (416,818 km³) of lava had flowed out, the rift had not only stopped expanding but was filled in. Magma had been flowing in for 20 million years. In some places this layer of hardened lava lies five to 12 miles (8 to 20 km) thick. And all over the North Shore the black beaches and dark rocks that can be seen are this ancient lava. Sometimes it has weathered to gray, and sometimes it is reddish from iron content. (For another major continental rift, elsewhere on the planet, see chapter 4: Lake Baikal.)

The rifting at Lake Superior stopped only because some ancient mountains (eroded long ago and so no longer visible) were being shoved up to the east, and the tectonic force moving inland that formed them also pressed the rift shut.

THE FIRST BASIN

All the volcanic rock around Lake Superior is very heavy. As it flowed, it gradually compressed the land here. This depression made the future Lake Superior's first basin, which also lay in the lower area of the former rift. It was then about 350 miles (560 km) long and 250 miles (400 km) wide, a bit larger than the basin today. With the major volcanism over, this area lay in relative geologic quiet for the next 998 million years. As the Paleozoic epoch began, more than 500 million years ago, large land plants and vertebrates (animals with backbones) began to inhabit the planet. And climate also became quite variable, here and elsewhere.

WHAT HAPPENED NEXT

At the beginning of the *Mesozoic* (225 to 70 million years ago), what is now Lake Superior's basin was attached to Greenland and northern

OUIMET CANYON

This unusual and dramatic canyon north of Lake Superior, on the Canadian section of the North Shore (pronounced "we-met") requires more study by the geologists of the future. How on earth did this place form?

First, the particulars: The Ouimet Canyon's sheer walls are 350 feet (115 m) high (taller than a 40-story building), stand an average of 500 feet (165 m) apart, and extend like this for more than two miles (3 km). At the bottom, in the chilly shade of the dark walls 109 yards (100 m) down, live subarctic plants, such as tiny arctic wintergreens, sandworts, mosses, liverworts, and lichen. The nearest place they grow in this canyon lies 620 miles (1,000 km) north, in the true subarctic zone of the planet. They have been here since the glacier retreated. The deepest parts of this canyon floor still holds ice, under a few boulders, all year long.

Geologists agree on some elements of Ouimet Canyon's creation. It is not a typical canyon, cut out over millions of years by a river (the way the Grand Canyon was created by the Colorado River). They also agree that a shallow ocean present here about 1.5 billion years ago left sediments, which later hardened into shale. After that, pools of the molten lava that flowed during the time of the Mid-Continent Rift hardened and forced their way up into the shale, forming pancake-shaped rock layers called sills. As the softer shale eroded, some of these sills became exposed and began to crack.

It is what happened next, the actual formation of the canyon, that causes geologists to disagree. The most accepted theory is that, in the several pulses of glaciation, ice and water got into these cracks or fractures and loosened the rock. Gradually it eroded from above to make a channel that became the canyon.

A second theory is that the immense weight of the glacial ice over the cracked rock warped the rock and then broke the top layers in half suddenly. Then erosion over the eons caused the opening to enlarge.

A third approach suggests that meltwater from the dying glacier seeped down into the shale. It continued to run off underground (toward Lake Superior) until a tunnel formed in the softer rock under the harder shale lying over it. This "cave" gradually weakened its own "roof," until the rock roof collapsed. That opened the canyon. No one is certain which theory is correct.

Europe. During this period they separated, the warm world of the dinosaurs cooled, and the land here took up its present position. *Sediments* piled up and compressed, creating the stable *crust* under Lake Superior. The crust here is now 22 to 34 miles (35 to 55 km) thick depending upon the area of the lake that is examined.

As the *Cenozoic epoch* began (about 70 million years ago), the planet became home to mammals, flowering plant species became common, and the grasses spread. The Lake Superior basin, a lowland area, was home to many of these species, but it did not yet have water. That came from a glacier.

THE GLACIER

In contemporary times—for geologists that means the last 2 million years—the most important influence on Lake Superior has been glaciation. This was glacier country, and its footprint remains today. The lake is *Pleistocene epoch terrane*.

The glacier gradually brought sediments, shoving a layer of clay, sand, soil, pebbles, rocks, even house-sized boulders, to form a thick layer over the bedrock. Called *glacial till*, this overlay can lie 600 feet (183 m) deep in the Lake Superior region, up to 1.2 miles (2 km) deep when more recent sediments over it are included. It covers the bedrock over most of the region.

The layer is not uniform, however. Many of today's beaches on Lake Superior, and some of its highest land areas, lack this blanket of glacial till. There it has washed away or worn away, exposing the bedrock. This is why the bare ancient lava can be seen so easily, especially on the North Shore. Some of the darkish rocks have a scattering of small light areas within them. These are antique lava, solid rock that once was thick, molten lava seething with gas bubbles. The bubbles popped a billion years ago or so, when the rock cooled, leaving the lighter areas in the rock.

POSITION OF THE GLACIER

The broad area of North America covered by the glacier was larger than the size of Antarctica today. But, like a giant scoop of vanilla ice cream perched at the North Pole, the glacial ice "dripped" down farther south in some areas than others. Within the United States much of Montana escaped glaciation. New England and New York State were covered, however. Cape Cod is actually a ridge of glacial till called a *moraine* shoved out into the ocean, and the Hudson River valley is actually an old fjord.

Here in the country's northern mid-section, the glacier extended down the farthest south, covering the land almost to where the Mississippi River meets the Ohio River. The ice just missed one corner—southeastern Minnesota, southwestern Wisconsin, and northeast Iowa,

HOW FAST DOES THE EARTH MOVE?

The continental plates are indeed always moving—though not quickly. The Earth's larger plates rarely speed any faster than one inch (2 cm) per year. Smaller ones can chug along at 2.4 to 3.5 inches (6 to 9 cm) per year. The ocean floor splits and oozes out lava at about the same rates. Plate movement is a slow process, but it is incredibly important.

The movement adds up. The Alps, Himalayas, Rockies, and many other mountain ranges were shoved up gradually by collisions among these plates. And the whole ocean floor is "recycled" every 200 to 300 million years; the bottom rock plunging down into the *mantle* in one place and oozing up or blasting out volcanically in another place. The ultimate energy for the movement of the solid land of this planet comes from the heart of the Earth. Heat there in the mantle surges up in massive, seething, flowing, and churning plumes of melted rock. This process, plate tectonics, is actually a sign that the Earth is alive. This deep-Earth process, understood but not in sufficient detail, is actively studied by geologists.

on the way—now called the "driftless area." The current position of the major rivers of the Midwest is not an accident. They were once differently situated, but carved new channels as they filled with the massive volume of glacial meltwater, just as Lake Superior did.

THE GLACIER'S THICKNESS

Across Canada the glacial ice was about three miles (4.8 km) thick. In Duluth, Minnesota, at the western point of Lake Superior, its thickness was "only" two miles (3.2 km). This white ice crown was immensely heavy. Estimates are that its pressure on the land was about 290 tons on every square foot of the Lake Superior basin and environs. It actually pressed the crust of the planet down about 2,640 feet (805 m), forcing it into the mantle. This is one way that an "ice monster" remodels the land. (For the effects that remain today in the northern world from the weight of this ice, please see chapter 10: Great Slave Lake.)

Glaciers also change the landscape by scooping. Glaciers move, and, as they do, they shove and grind the rock away in front of them, even solid rock. They then push it along. The land under the present Lake Superior was lower to begin with, and it became yet lower from the weight of the ice. Then it was "shoveled" out in this way, becoming even lower.

GLACIAL STAGES

The Pleistocene was not solid ice all the time. Glaciers built Lake Superior in several stages, each white pulse lasting 60,000 to 75,000 years. A melting phase after each buildup lasted 15,000 to 20,000 years. Then warmer periods between, with little or no glaciation, lasted 200,000 to 300,000 years apiece. The last maximum of the glacier at Lake Superior was 18,000 years ago. By 10,000 years ago, it was retreating. The sluice of meltwater overwhelmed drainage areas and made the rivers keep changing shape and position. Lake Superior reached its present position and size only about 9,500 years ago.

Glaciation largely ended worldwide between 11,000 and 6,000 years ago, depending upon location. Only in Greenland, Antarctica, and scattered mountain valleys elsewhere does it remain today. We are, right now, in the fourth warm, "interglacial" period of the Pleistocene.

All these numbers are rough, and *paleogeologists* (geologists whose field is *paleogeology*) are still studying the glaciation process intensely. Melting took longer where the ice was thicker. There are also local differences and even short periods of ice growth within warming periods. Much remains to be researched.

Will there be another blast of glaciation? There have, after all, been 12 "ice ages" in Earth's history, with the Pleistocene only the most recent one during the last 2 million years. This issue will be discussed in chapter 6: Lake Vänern and chapter 10: Great Slave Lake.

LAKE LEVELS

During the retreats of the glacier here at Lake Superior, the depth of the lake's water changed radically. Warmer temperatures meant more evaporation, but they also often meant more snowfall (which then melts). Lake levels have also changed since the last melt. There have been three major high-water times, called "highstands," here called the Nipissing I, Nipissing II, and Algoma. Lake Nipigon, an immense lake just north of Lake Superior in Canada, was part of the main lake during these periods. These highstands can be traced, roughly, by looking at which plants were growing where, and analyzed by looking at the fossil pollen remaining. Among the many topics geologists are studying is to what extent climate change has been responsible for these variations. (For more on pollen analysis, see chapter 1: Caspian Sea.)

Sand dunes can also be "fossil" evidence of the water's height in a given place, since many are ancient beaches. This is tricky geology for many reasons, among them the fact that dunes can also wash away entirely. But geologists can find ancient plants and tree stumps buried deep within dunes and also look for soil layers created as the high water destroyed bluffs near the lake.

On the South Shore of Lake Superior, the Grand Sable Dunes rise as high as 295 feet (90 m) above the lake's current water level and cover four square miles (10 km²) with hilly sand. They seem to show four to 11 different highstands of Lake Superior in that area over the last 5,500 years. The Nodaway Dunes, also on the South Shore, are known to be between 3,000 and 4,000 years old.

On the South Shore of Lake Superior, Pulpit Rock is within Michigan's wooded Presque Isle Park. *(Library of Congress, Prints & Photographs Division, Detroit Publishing Company)*

Sand dunes and ridges can be found even underwater in Lake Superior. In the southwestern area of the lake, off Wisconsin, a group of stable sandy ridges has been located under the lake's surface about 1.8 miles (3 km) offshore. The deep gullies within them, and the fact that they are not lined up the way the waves now run, tell geologists that they have been here for a long time. One cluster of ridges extends for more than 1.2 miles (2 km) and covers a .3-mile-wide (.5-km-wide) area, with each ridge rising 10 to 16 feet (3 to 5 m) high. These underwater sand features were probably formed by currents or storms when the lake was about 33 feet (10 m) lower than it is today.

Two other types of glacial "footprint" can be seen around Lake Superior, too. On some areas of exposed bedrock, groups of narrow scratches —perhaps .2 inch (.5 cm) deep—run roughly parallel across the rock face. These were made by sharp rocks embedded in the bottom of the glacier—the rocks "wrote" like pencils on the underlying rock as the glacier moved across. And sometimes you can see glacial *potholes*, like whirlpools carved into solid rock. Now empty or holding a bit of rain, these potholes were made by the violent force of rivers swollen with glacial meltwater. The powerful rivers carried a lot of rock slurry, and eddies of pebbles actually carved the potholes out of solid rock. (For more on glacial potholes, see chapter 10: Great Slave Lake.)

The glacier is gone but not forgotten at Lake Superior. Its evidence is everywhere. In fact, most of the water in Lake Superior today is still melted ice from the glacier. And the land at its eastern edge, around Sault Ste. Marie (on the Ontario-Michigan border) is still continuing to rise a little from its weight. (For a discussion of this phenomenon, see chapter 10: Great Slave Lake.)

ORES

Lake Superior, part of the vast Canadian Shield formation of ancient granite and other rock from the Precambrian, is home to some of the richest and most significant metallic ores in the world, all courtesy of its geology. An ore is a mixture of ordinary rock and valuable metal.

The largest, most famous iron ore deposits in the entire world lie here on the North Shore. Mining them has created fortunes—and lost some, too. The rich copper ores of the Keweenaw Peninsula on the South Shore, now mostly mined out, were once also the largest of their kind in the world. The Native Americans had begun mining copper on Isle Royale and Micipicoten Island, for example, as early as 5,000 years ago. Silver has also been mined in the region, with extremely valuable deposits near Thunder Bay on the Canadian North Shore. A brief gold rush also occurred in the Superior region, and a new one began in the Minnesota stretch of the North Shore in 2004, but not nearly as much gold has been found here compared to the other minerals. (The Canadian North Shore has much more gold.)

LAKE SUPERIOR V. LAKE MALAWI

Most people would guess that the northerly Lake Superior and the tropical Lake Malawi, a three-million year old *rift valley* lake in Africa, though both very large, are quite different. This is true—and a great deal of the difference lies in their light budgets.

Lake Malawi receives sunshine for so much more of the year that it becomes much richer in *plankton*, which thicken the water's appearance. Down deeper in Malawi, the water becomes lower in nitrogen and higher in phosphorous, and the layers of the lake do not mix as well as do Lake Superior's. These elements choke out the oxygen, leading to the growth of certain bacteria, which then make the lake greener and soupier. The chronically lower oxygen levels also allow the phosphorous to attach to certain metals in the water—and this, in turn, leads to faster erosion of soils at the shoreline.

Lake Superior receives far less light than Lake Malawi, and has far less life within it. This is one big reason why its water is much clearer than Lake Malawi's.

The rocks that became these ores began to form about 2 billion years ago, as seafloor *sediments*. Gradually, the sediments compacted and became about 30 percent iron. This is a very high percentage. There are plenty of ores being mined around the world with metal concentrations of only a few percent. Iron ore is the raw material used to make steel and so is quite valuable.

The next stage of ore formation involved the hot, liquid pulses of *volcanism* during the time when the Mid-Continent Rift was forming. The lava melted the rock around it, and often the metals in them then flowed together and cooled together. Iron began to concentrate especially richly in an area inland from the northwestern part of Lake Superior.

Then a bit more than 100 million years ago the ore here became even more concentrated, up to 90 percent iron! In the 1890s an immense deposit was discovered by two men, the Merritt brothers, from Duluth, Minnesota. They formed a mining company to exploit this resource, building whole railway systems to transport it. Other people joined the industry and tried to buy them out. The Merritts once turned down an offer of $8 million (worth at least twice as much today). After the Panic of 1893, however, the economic downturn made them go broke—and they had to sell out to John D. Rockefeller for very little money. Rockefeller, Andrew Carnegie, James J. Hill, and J. P. Morgan eventually formed U.S. Steel, a major corporation, on the basis of this "mother lode" of ore, all thanks to the geology of Lake Superior.

The iron ore called taconite is still being mined and processed here today. One of the main reasons for all the shipping in Lake Superior is the transportation of these processed ores across the lake to the steel mills of Pennsylvania and the world. (Many of the large shipwrecks have been these of giant ore boats.)

WATER QUALITY

The mining industry around Lake Superior damages the water quality of the lake. Effluents include asbestoslike particles from the taconite "tailings," leftovers dumped from the processing of this iron-rich resource.

Though this is of concern, more significant are the airborne pollutants, most arriving from quite far away, and, to a lesser extent, contaminants entering via the many rivers. Air masses from the south, which arrive at times in the summer even to such a northerly place, bring DDT all the way up from Mexico; in that country it is still legal to spray crops with this dangerous pesticide. Nitrates, a fertilizer, come in from faraway agricultural operations, on airborne dust.

Mercury also blows into Lake Superior from coal-burning power plants as far away as the Pacific Northwest (prevailing winds are out of the west). Though air and water concentrations of mercury are low, the metal accumulates quickly in fish—small fish are eaten by bigger fish, which are then eaten by even bigger fish. The mercury can become concentrated many thousands of times. It has reached a level where one should not eat Lake Superior fish more than once a week, since mercury can become a toxin to the human brain. Mercury has also been found in deer mice on Isle Royale, far out in the lake off Canada.

Toxaphene (a pesticide), however, is probably the most significant contaminant in Lake Superior's water, even though it has long been banned in this country. Polycyclic aromatic hydrocarbons (PAHs), herbicides such as atrazine and polychlorinated biphenyls (PCBs), chlordane, and hydrophobic organochlorine pesticides such as deldrin and lindane are also present in the water, though not at high levels. PCBs have been decreasing gradually in the lake since its usage was banned in the late 1970s. This chemical stew does not affect water clarity, but its effects are there.

Lake Superior has no large cities on it or even nearby, which helps to keep pollution levels quite low when compared to most other lakes in the United States. Suspended particles in its water attach to some of the metal particles, which drift in it. As they sink together, the deep, cold sediments on the lake's bottom can "entomb" pollutants, keeping them out of circulation to a certain extent.

But the low water temperatures here mean that organisms, which could absorb yet more pollutants, do not grow or proliferate quickly. And there are fewer of them to die and build up the sediment level that sops them up. Natural recycling of anything in Lake Superior takes a long time.

This lake, however, is so much cleaner than the Caspian Sea and the Aral Sea (subjects of the previous two chapters) that comparisons are ludicrous. It is also cleaner than the rest of the Great Lakes. Depending upon where you live, this lake may be cleaner than what comes out of a faucet.

IN THE FIELD: MERCURY TESTING

Mercury is one focus of geological study here since not enough is known about how it accumulates in the fish and other wildlife. The water itself does have quite low levels of this hazardous metal, but the small fishing industry and the much larger tourism industry are concerned about the safety of the fish.

To assess levels, geologists motor out in a research vessel (owned by their university or a government agency) equipped with mesh nets, sieves, a pump, a benthic grab (to collect bottom sediments), portable freezers, and other equipment. Towing the mesh behind the boat, they can collect plankton from several different areas of the lake; they freeze it right on board for study back in their labs. They also pump large volumes of lake water through a series of sieves to collect more plankton from the top half inch to two inches (1 to 5 cm) of water, again in their search for mercury. The particles collected are dried and then filtered in various ways back in the lab. Bottom-dwelling organisms are grabbed, rinsed, and freeze-dried also.

Analysis requires heating, filtering, and then examining the material through *gas chromatography*, a technique in which geologists vaporize a sample of the material to detect the chemicals in it. PCBs and trace metals besides mercury are analyzed in this way also.

Among the many findings by various groups of geologists is that the area of Lake Superior off Thunder Bay, Ontario, has the highest concentration of mercury within Lake Superior, though that mercury pollution has been decreasing even here. (There was more mercury in the lake in 1973 than there is now.)

IN THE FIELD: LIGHT BUDGETS

Another area of research in Lake Superior is its light budget, the amount of light the lake receives over a day or over a year. Light is one of the key determinants of the nature of a lake, creating the most major difference between a northerly lake like this one and a tropical lake. Tropical lakes receive much more uniform light across a year, and even throughout a day, than Lake Superior does.

Light is, after all, solar energy, the engine that drives the lake's metabolism, broadly defined. It affects not only the creatures that live in the lake but also the layering of the lake and the circulation of its waters. Light during the day, which warms a lake, is then lost as heat when night comes. This difference actually changes the weight of the water slightly and aids its circulation. (Lake circulation or "turnover" will be discussed in more detail in chapter 4: Lake Baikal.)

The amount of light reaching the lake is extremely variable in Lake Superior. The top six and a half feet (2 m) generally absorb more than half of the incoming light, and the first three feet (1 m) generally transform more than half of that light into heat. But Lake Superior's water clarity means that more light penetrates deeper down than in most lakes. (This happens because there are fewer particles suspended in the water to scatter the light than there are in most lakes.) Lake Superior also has fewer aquatic plants near the shore; these block 50 to 90 percent of the light in many lakes. So Superior's light budget is quite positive.

When winter arrives, there are fewer hours of daylight, and the ice cover builds. Though black ice actually emits about as much light as regular water, white ice does not. Also called popcorn ice, white ice gets its color from the many air bubbles, irregular snow crystals, and absorbed snow within it. A thick, bumpy, snow-covered white ice blocks the most light of all, reflecting 75 to 95 percent of it away from the lake. (In summer waves can be bumpy enough to reflect some light away but not nearly this much.)

While the lack of winter light here can injure or kill many organism, fish live all winter under the ice layer of Lake Superior. Air pollutants can make the available light dangerous, however, allowing more ultraviolet light to penetrate the lake. Though algae are able to repair their genetic material every night, most creatures are not very resilient when encountering ultraviolet light. Fortunately, air pollution levels here are pretty low.

Lake Superior's light profile is studied most basically by the use of a *Secchi disk*. A white disk at the bottom of a rope marked with measurement lines, this low-tech tool is dropped slowly into the lake until it can no longer be seen—because there is not enough light. That point is then read from the rope measurement at the surface and recorded. When measurements are done the same way at many different places and during many different conditions, a profile of the lake's light can be constructed mathematically. (For more on Secchi disk measurements, see chapter 8: Crater Lake.)

THE LAKE IN THE WORLD

Lake Superior is a major avenue for water commerce. Each year about 44 million tons (40 million metric tons) of cargo move out of the "Port of Duluth," Minnesota, and nearby Superior, Wisconsin. Ships carry cargo to destinations on the other Great Lakes such as Chicago and Cleveland and to the world beyond. Close to two-thirds of all the steel made in the United States begins as iron ore, geologically created and now carried by ships across Lake Superior. In Duluth the vessels that traverse the oceans, as opposed to remaining within the Great Lakes, are called "salties."

These salties bring business, but they also bring "invasive species," creatures not native to Lake Superior or to the Great Lakes but that happen to be able to live and reproduce here once they arrive. These invaders are occasionally attached to the hulls of the ships coming in from the ocean, but they have usually traveled more comfortably, in the "ballast water." This is the water held low in the ship, in its hold, pumped in there to keep the ship efficiently balanced as it moves. Ballast water is added by the shipping companies at any convenient port. Small organisms from as far away as the Caspian Sea, called euryhalines, have arrived and now live in Lake Superior. So do other migrants. Some of them end up eating up some of Lake Superior's own inhabitants.

This lake's creatures cannot live without freshwater, which is fortunately abundant in Lake Superior. For more than 20 years, the governors of the Great Lakes states, along with the provincial leaders of Ontario and Quebec (on the St. Lawrence Seaway) have been trying to settle on a policy to regulate water withdrawals from Lake Superior, as "water rights." These rights address the following questions: Who is allowed to draw out and drink—or sell—this water? How much of it can be removed safely? Must it be cleaned and returned by some industries? Whose state or national laws should govern? The policy has not yet been completely decided, and it is a source of real conflict today. Geologists who study the history of lake levels and the ways groundwater enters the lake are among those who contribute to this issue as it evolves.

The Great Lakes taken together hold 5,906 cubic miles (24,620 km^3) of water and cover 94,688 square miles (245,240 km^2). Only 253 lakes found on the whole planet are larger than 193 square miles (500 km^2) apiece, a tiny fraction of Lake Superior's own size of 32,160 square miles (83,300 km^2). This is an important place for the planet, a big drink of water created by a huge slab of ice.

Lake Superior is the most extensive expanse of freshwater in the world. Cold and clean compared to other lakes, it acts as an air conditioner for the surrounding towns and small cities. Because of its depth and size, storms here can be deadly.

4

Lake Baikal

Central Asia

Lake Baikal, in Russia's southeastern Siberia, is an immense, deep, cold-water *terrain*, shaped like a sideways exclamation mark without the dot. It shares significant superlatives with Lake Superior. Superior is the freshwater lake with the greatest surface area of any in the world, and Baikal is the freshwater lake with the greatest volume of water on the planet. In fact Lake Baikal holds more water than all the Great Lakes poured together, an estimated 20 percent of all the surface freshwater on the planet. (That does not include groundwater, atmospheric water, or, of course, the oceans, always salt water.) Baikal's water adds up to an impressive 14,000 cubic miles (58,355 km^3).

All of this water lies in a lake "only" about as large as Switzerland. Baikal is just under 400 miles (645 km) long and between 20 and 50 miles (32 and 80 km) wide. Its coastline stretches 525 miles (845 km) along the western side and 640 miles (1,030 km) along its eastern shore.

DEPTH

Lake Baikal contains so much water in a basin that is less broad than Superior's because it is so dramatically deep. This is the deepest lake in the world, about a mile down in several locations and almost that deep on average, since the sides of its basin plunge down so steeply. There are 200-foot (60-m) "drop-offs" near shore, and, even nearer, where it may be "only" 30 feet (9 m) deep, fairly large ships can approach conveniently close to the land. The lake's maximum depth is 5,317 feet (1,637 m).

To get some idea of the amount of freshwater in this lake, think about rivers for a moment. Ponder first the Amazon, which pours out enough water—every day—to equal the water usage of the whole United States. Picture Lake Baikal empty. Then turn on the faucet of the Amazon. Next, open the faucets of every other river and stream on the planet. Direct all this water to flow into Lake Baikal's empty basin. It would take about a year to fill it up.

In November Lake Baikal and its environs steadily freeze. The mountains north of the lake are already completely covered in snow. *(NASA, Visible Earth)*

COLD AND WILD TERRAIN

Lake Baikal is also dramatically cold. In winter parts of the lake can freeze to 33 feet (10 m) down, and spring moves slowly to melt this ice. Its *watershed* is mostly mountains, which add their load of cold snowmelt in springtime. More than 300 rivers, usually almost as chilly, pour into the lake. Rocky shores can be seen in the color insert on page C-3.

The area close to the lake is steep in most areas. The mountains surrounding Baikal are 4,600 to 6,000 feet (1,400 to 1,830 m) high, covered in forest. The rest of the shoreline includes deltas where the largest rivers enter (the Selenga, Kichera, and Angara), an area of rolling grassland called grassy "steppes," two cities (Irkutsk and Ulan-Ude), and some towns. People have lived along this lake for at least 5,000 years, possibly for 9,000 years, hunting and fishing, long before the days of these cities.

Three national parks, each about the size of Yellowstone, lie near its edges, too, along with four other wilderness areas just as large. There are hot springs in places. The nearby forest is "taiga," dark from all the northern evergreens, though lightened in places by stands of birch and aspen. Wild berries and mushrooms abound. The lake has been classified as a World Heritage Site by UNESCO (United Nations Educational, Scientific and Cultural Organization) because its unique characteristics are so worth preserving.

Except on the south end (near Irkutsk and the Mongolian border), where logging and paper mills, along with some mining, have polluted the lake, Lake Baikal is very clean. In its northern expanses, people drink water directly from the lake. Whether this situation can safely continue will be discussed later in the chapter.

THE "GALÁPAGOS" OF RUSSIA

Lake Baikal is rich in wildlife. Through its clear water, near shore, scuba divers can see green sponges on the bottom and the flickers of myriad fish. About 56 species of fish swim through the lake, more than 1,000 species of water plants live in it, and splashing around is the Baikal seal called the nerpa or yerpa; it is the only entirely freshwater seal in the world. Deep down live multicolored worms up to one foot (30 cm) long, along with about 140 different species of flatworms. Another inhabitant is the golomyanka, a deepwater fish that can withstand water pressures that would crush other living things. This might be the most biologically diverse lake on the planet.

Lake Baikal's mountains are home to bears that weigh nearly 1,500 pounds (680 kg). Flying near one might be a capercailliye, a grouse about the size of a turkey that can live on pine needles alone. It buries itself in the snow to keep warm in wintertime.

Lake Baikal is called the "Galápagos" of Russia since both are relatively isolated places and important outposts of evolution. (The Galápagos are islands off Ecuador in South America.) At Baikal more than 80 percent of the more than 1,200 animal species and more than 600 of the plants are *endemic;* that means that they are found nowhere else in the world, having evolved here. Scientists working at this lake discover about 20 new species per year, many of them endemic. Life has had ample time here for evolution. More on this subject is found later in the chapter.

OLDEST BUT STILL NEW

To add another blue ribbon prize to a blue lake, Lake Baikal is the oldest lake in the world, since it formed between 30 million and 15 million years ago. Since only about a dozen freshwater lakes on the planet are even as old as 18,000 to 9,000 years, this record may well be its most amazing of all. The lake was formed *tectonically,* here by the pulling apart of the Earth's crustal *plates.* Over eons that has made a deep *rift valley.* The

---

AN EVEN COLDER—BUT INVISIBLE—LAKE

An immense lake exists on Earth that is colder even than Lake Baikal, but no one has ever seen it. It is about the size of Lake Ontario, its deepest point nearly 1,800 feet (550 m) down. Its bottom layers are—strangely—warmer than its top layers. This is Lake Vostok. Highly unusual, Vostok lies under a two-mile- (3.2-km-) thick blanket of ice—in Antarctica.

Geologists discovered their first evidence of Lake Vostok about 40 years ago. By chance they had built a research station on the ice right on top of it. They were doing seismic studies, in which electronic waves are directed down then analyzed as they come back up. In this method geologists can "see" the intervening materials. It looked as though a lake was down there! Radar pulses from an airborne lab and later from a satellite finally confirmed the lake's existence in 1993. (For more on the use of seismic waves, please see chapter 1: Caspian Sea and chapter 8: Crater Lake.)

The only reason that a liquid water lake can exist in Antarctica at all is that heat from the Earth's *core,* "exhaled" up through the *mantle,* must be keeping the water from freezing the whole way down from the icy air above its "surface." Vostok may, in fact, lie in a deep rift valley the way Baikal does. Much remains to be studied here.

Vostok can remain liquid since it is under a protective thick lid of ice, which keeps the dramatically cold surface air of Antarctica away. Though summer in parts of Antarctica can mean some open streams, as a bit of the ice and snow melt, there are no open expanses of water that could be called lakes on this continent. There are, however, other, smaller invisible lakes, under their ice "lids," that have also been discovered. More than 145 of these have now been found, some of them linked.

So far, geologists have drilled into the ice above the water level of Lake Vostok and found frozen bacteria. They suspect that microorganisms of some sort, and conceivably larger creatures, might live underneath the permanent ice, in the liquid water. If so, this could indicate that there might also be life on some of the frozen planets and moons elsewhere in our solar system. Vostok's ancient water and sediments could also hold clues to ancient climate shifts on Earth.

Lake Vostok's organisms, if any, would have evolved long, long before humans walked the Earth, back when Antarctica entered its deep-freeze. These organisms would be an important resource that should not be contaminated by microbes from the surface world. For this reason geologists' drilling and coring equipment has been directed into the ice but has not yet probed the liquid water levels of the lake. They are first trying to figure out a wise way to do this.

valley, now filled by Baikal's water, is the deepest continental depression on the planet (only the ocean floor is more deeply rifted, in places).

The Baikal area is still geologically active, the rifting going on even today. The lake's basin continues to widen along the rifted bottom by .12 to .2 inch (3 to 5 mm) per year, and the bottom is still dropping by about .8 inch (20 mm) per year. So Lake Baikal, filled by many rivers and emptied only by the Angara, should continue to get deeper and deeper, holding a greater and greater volume of water. Even the normal filling in of the lake's basin by river silt and other run-off *sediments*—which gradually ends the life of many lakes—is insignificant here compared to the geological deepening.

The *tectonic activity* at Lake Baikal is marked by more than 2,000 small earthquakes every year, noted at area monitoring stations, as the ground fractures. The rifting at Baikal, the most active on a continental plate, has been studied intensively by geologists.

RIFTING

In *Paleozoic* days (500 to 270 million years ago), a small, shallow lake existed here, but the true origins of Lake Baikal began "only" between 35 and 30 million years ago.

The rifting, or pulling apart of the crustal plates of the planet, accelerated here in earnest since then. As a basin formed, it began to fill with water, then more rifting came, then more water, and the process continued in this way. The rifting was accompanied by uplift, raising the

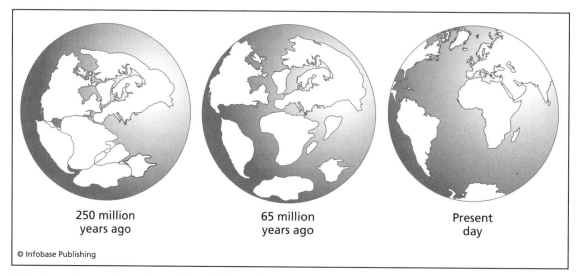

250 million
years ago

65 million
years ago

Present
day

© Infobase Publishing

This schematic map shows the position of the continents going back about 200 million years, with the Lake Baikal area always very northerly.

RIFT VALLEY LAKE, ASIAN LAKE

As can be seen with Lake Baikal, a lake created by *tectonic rifting* is likely to be very deep. In the cases where deep rifts are seen on land, they look like sharp-edged valleys. So lakes of this kind are often called rift valley lakes.

Lake Tanganyika, quite ancient at 9 to 12 million years old, fills one long section of the Great Rift Valley in southeastern Africa, and is called a rift valley lake. It comes in second to Lake Baikal in water volume on the planet. Tanganyika stretches more than 400 miles (650 km) long, as much as 30 miles (50 km) wide, and more than .62 mile (1 km) deep in places. That makes room for a lot of water.

This lake comes in second to Lake Baikal in another dimension also: It contains about half the number of species and subspecies as Baikal does, which is still a large amount. But unlike Baikal, it appears to be both warming and its water layers becoming less thoroughly mixed at spring and fall turnover.

Another interesting lake, Lake Koko-Nor, is an Asian neighbor of Lake Baikal. If one drew a straight line east from the middle of the Caspian Sea to an area almost directly south of Lake Baikal, that point would be near Lake Koko-Nor. This large lake is interesting because it is so high in elevation, 10,515 feet (3,205 m), in the Nan Mountains of China, part of the vast Himalayan area. It is quite large, 65 miles (105 km) long, 40 miles (65 km) wide, and it expands and shrinks significantly depending upon snowmelt and rain.

Not as large as Baikal but a beautiful Asian lake, Koko-Nor's shores are inhabited by Mongolians and Tibetans. It is an excellent frontier for geological research since it has been little studied by geologists so far.

mountains that surround nearly the whole lake. This uplifting continues today, just as the rifting does. Both have directed and redirected the rivers (rivers amid changing mountains must shift to find the lowest ground), as well as deepening the basin.

Another factor that makes this lake unusual is that the area's tectonic forces do not ever seem to have paused here for very long. The last 3 million years have been quite active. At around 2.65 million years ago tectonic activity seems to have been especially intense, deepening this underwater gash in the planet's crust significantly.

And, in the last million years or so, even more has happened geologically. The central part of the rift under the lake has shoved westward, while another flank continues to move south. The "shoulders" of the massive rifted rocks tilt upward and downward in various places under the lake's surface. The underwater ridges that result can be up to 125 miles (200 km) long. This local shaping of the lake bottom is the reason Lake Baikal has three especially deep areas within its basin. The lake is more complex than a simple slash in the ground, gradually deepening across the millennia, but it can also be thought of that way.

SHOVING AROUND THE EDGES

Lake Baikal lies in a general area that is especially geologically active, though at the same time it is quite near a very stable area of the Earth's crust. The large, more stationery swatch (to the north) is called the Siberian Craton or Shield. Typically, the crust around a craton, an area called the *mobile belt*, experiences a great deal of tectonic activity. The more mobile, moving pieces of the crust are shoving against the craton, but find it too large and hard and deep to move. So they push into one another instead. This makes for plenty of "Earth-action."

Over the eons the North America and Eurasia plates have converged here, and another plate, the Amur, has pushed southeast into northeastern Asia, and other such collisions have happened. Forces like these can easily create cracks—the rifts—in the crust. Major earthquakes have left evidence like this at Lake Baikal for at least 25 million years.

Along with the Baikal rift, other major rifting areas on the continents of the world include ones in the southern Rhine River area of Germany and France, the rift in Kenya in which Lake Tanganyika is found, and the Rio Grande rift between the Texas and Mexico. The failed rift associated with Lake Superior is discussed in that chapter.

TWO KINDS OF RIFTING HERE

Geologists continue to study the Lake Baikal rift and the others mentioned above to decide whether they are more "active" or more "passive" rifts. Active ones feature massive plumes of molten rock that well up within the crack. More passive ones are created when dramatic volcanic upwelling reaches the surface, but where no more complex, broader-scale collisions exist to shape the activity on the rift.

There is a need for more research here—especially an analysis of small rock features within Lake Baikal's deep rift—to see how many of them are upwelled material from deep within the Earth. More study of the geological history of the surrounding mountains is also needed. But it looks now as though Baikal is a relatively passive rift.

Passive does not mean quiet, however. The Lake Baikal area is tremendously active seismically, with small earthquakes almost all the time. There are also vents at places on the lake bottom, as will be discussed later in the chapter.

RIFTS AND GLACIERS

Though it may seem as though the dramatic and extensive rifting that created the Lake Baikal basin might have nothing to do with the process of glaciation in the mountainous area here, the two are indeed related. And, taken together, they are the major forces that have written the area's history, though the lake itself does not seem ever to have been fully glaciated. (It is too far south.) The reason is that the rifting, which created the mountains along with the lake's basin, thereby shaped the weather.

Mountains that have built up in one area of the world, as here, cannot throw a whole planet into an ice age—that broader process is discussed in chapter 3: Lake Superior, chapter 6: Lake Vänern, and chapter 10: Great Slave Lake—but they can make a huge difference locally. Here the intense rifting period that was centered around 2.65 million years ago was at about the same time as one period of glaciation in Siberia to the north.

The interplay between mountain building and glaciation goes this way. The new mountains block and divert the winds, which bring additional storms (see chapter 1: Caspian Sea and chapter 5: Lake Titicaca for sections on the *rainshadows* of mountains for how this happens). The storms allow more snow to accumulate in the area. The more extensive snowfields—accumulating most readily in the mountain valleys as valley glaciers—then reflect heat back into the atmosphere (instead of absorbing it, as darker ground does). That chills the local climate further, and the process accelerates. Warmer periods come in between the much colder ones, of course, and as the ice on the lake melts, methane is released from the lake sediments. That intensifies the warming pulse. (Methane is a greenhouse gas which, in the atmosphere, acts to warm the planet, and it is produced by rotting organic-rich sediments, among other ways.) So both cooling and warming forces accelerate, but the mountains tip the balance toward cooling.

Both the rifting here at Baikal and vast Siberian ice to the north also changed the course of the rivers coming in and out of Lake Baikal. A huge new area of rock or ice in a different place can make a river flow along an altered path, even in a quite different direction for a long stretch. The lake level dropped here occasionally as a result of this kind of change, but scientists think that Baikal was probably always the world's deepest lake.

GLACIATION SHAPES BAIKAL

Though rifting created the deep basin of Lake Baikal, glaciers have continually altered the shape of its environs in the high elevations as they pressed down hills and mountains, scooped out valleys, shoved ice down to alter shorelines, left rubble fields, and created other local features. Glacial actions can be read in the "neighborhood" rocks, and, since the lake is so old (30 to 15 million years old), the record goes far back. Geologists have been able to analyze glaciation in Siberia as far back as 10 to 12 million years. (Before that, the glacial record becomes difficult to read.)

As evidence of these changes, ancient beach lines can be found on and around Lake Baikal, and also under its present water level. Some can be spotted because they are *moraines*—lines of rock, rocky material, and sand shoved along by a glacier but then left in place as it melted. The stalled ridge of rocky material marks where the ice stopped. Some of these features cover areas as much as 1.2 miles (2 km) in diameter and extend as far into the present lake as 12.5 miles (20 km) in places.

The first pulse of glaciation in the Baikal area's higher elevations might have been as long ago as 4 to 3⅓ million years (though the cooling had begun gradually at 7 to 6 million years ago). Winter snow in a cooling period lasts all year long, and its levels pile up. The snow layers can gradually compress and crystallize into ice, making a glacier. Another pulse of glaciation slapped its white slab of ice over parts of this area about 2.8 to 2.6, or 2.5 million years ago, perhaps beginning its cooling a few hundred thousand years before that. Other glacial pulses have been dated at about 1.8 to 1.6 million years ago, 50,000 years ago, 40,000 to 35,000 years ago, 26,000 to 13,000 and 8,000 to 5,000 years ago. In between these periods of intense glaciation at higher elevations, the glaciers melted or partly melted, and snow fell only or mostly in winter. Sometimes the shift between colder periods and warmer periods was gradual and sometimes more abrupt.

Glaciers alter the land and they are also altered by it, since, like ice rivers, they will detour around uplifted sections of the rift or around areas of especially hard rock. These glacial paths can also be figured out. More about how this information is gathered and analyzed by geologists will be discussed in the "In the Field" sections at the end of the chapter.

WHY GLACIERS?

Though the rifting and uplifting of mountains in the Lake Baikal area affected the path of the glaciers, the tectonic changes that have gone on here, and are still going on, are too slow to have actually caused the many pulses of glaciation. Glaciers have additional causes.

Geologists have studied this intensively and continue to do so today. They begin their analysis by charting the known times of glaciation worldwide, though with far more knowledge about the "recent" glacial period called the Pleistocene (from about 2 million years ago through now). We are now in a warm period within this epoch; the last peak of glaciation was about 20,000 years ago, and most of the melting on Earth ended only about 9,000 years ago.

Next come the theories, and they involve the whole planet. Two broad factors involving complex cycles of tilts and wobbles seem to create the major climate changes that cause glaciers. They do so by affecting the amount of solar radiation, the heat from the Sun, that reaches us. The first is a 100,000-year cycle, called the Milankovitch cycle. It is caused by slight changes in the shape of the Earth's orbit around the

Sun, a tilt that draws us closer or farther at different times. Another such change seems to occur in a 400,000-year cycle. The next factor is a small wobble in the axis of the Earth. This wobble, called a *precession*, occurs in cycles of about 23,000 years, with a variant of it occurring in a 41,000-year cycle. The wobbles tilt the Northern Hemisphere either slightly more toward the Sun or slightly more away from it and the Southern Hemisphere in the other direction, enough to make a difference.

These cyclic changes are small, but they do affect the amount of solar radiation, or heat, that reaches a hemisphere of our planet. After all, it takes a drop in average temperature of only 4 to 9°F (–15.5° to –13°C), present over time, to create a period of glaciation.

HEAT FORCES

Now that the ice has retreated from the Lake Baikal area, it is possible to ponder the way local heat patterns affect the geology of the lake. Immediately, this lake earns another superlative: Baikal is the largest freshwater lake in the world with *hydrothermal vents*. These are cracks in the rocky, sedimented lake bottom that spew out hot water or steam—it is about 24°F (–4°C) warmer than the chilly water around them. At Baikal's underwater "spas" live luminous bacteria that grow in mats, see-through shrimp and other crustaceans in pink, worms (one with a yellowish green stomach), snails, bone white sponges the shape of mushrooms, white mollusks, and fish that can live in incessant and total darkness. All of them get their food and energy not from the Sun, as most creatures on the planet do, but from the chemistry of the hot water.

The vent area at Baikal lies in the northern section of the lake, at a depth of 1,350 feet (412 m). Scientists discovered it by descending in a submersible, equipped with very bright headlights. To decide where to descend, they had looked beforehand for spikes in temperature, using mechanical probes dropped from the surface down to the bottom in various places.

FUTURE OCEAN?

The geology of a lake with hydrothermal vents is at least as interesting as its biology. Vents like these, associated with rifting, are also found at long ridges on the floors of the oceans where crustal plates of the planet are pushing apart. (This is the main way the Atlantic Ocean has formed and is widening today.) Scientists already know that rifting is widening Lake Baikal and that this rift extends through Baikal. It is also much longer even than the lake.

These active hydrothermal vents could indicate a new ocean in the making. If the splitting continues, the continent would eventually crack open here. Ocean water would flow in if the rifting reached that far. (To learn about how this process started, but then stopped, see chapter 3: Lake Superior.)

One of the many areas where future geologists can contribute at Lake Baikal is by figuring out how long this rifting might continue. They will do this by further analyzing the plumes of molten rock in the core and mantle of the Earth. That is the "motor" that keeps plate tectonics going, as is known; but why a plume continues to seethe under a particular place is not well understood at all.

HEAT LAYERING

The vents at the bottom of a lake as immense as Lake Baikal do not contribute significantly to the stratification, or heat layering of the lake. Baikal is a turbulent lake in a location with very pronounced differences between winter and summer. The cycles of freezing and thawing power changes among water layers all the way down to the bottom, though the lower layers of the lake change less. Overall, Lake Baikal mixes its water layers about as often as the ocean does. Upper layers go down and lower layers come up, like flipping a pancake, but much slower and with stirring of the batter. Why?

The engine of lake stratification, or heat layering is, at its basis, the Sun. On a warm, sunny day, the top layer, or *epilimnion*, of a lake heats up. In a very small shallow northern lake, of just 10 acres perhaps, the Sun usually heats the water all the way down to the bottom, eliminating heat stratification. But in deeper lakes, and certainly in Baikal, stratification is very dynamic, especially in spring and fall. The deeper water remains much colder than the water layers near the surface.

HOW THIS WORKS: SPRING "TURNOVER"

The "turnover" of a lake's layers actually happens. It happens in spring and fall in temperate zones of the planet. In spring, to begin with, the water's density changes with the water's temperature, and water is most dense (heaviest) at 39°F (4°C). As the temperature of the water increases beyond this point, because of the Sun's warmth, it becomes less dense (lighter). Lighter levels rise, and heavier levels sink. This process freshens the lake by allowing the lower water to interact with the greater flow of oxygen across the surface. Wind ripples and waves cause further mixing. The oxygenation of the water helps nurture living things in the lake and hastens the decomposition of the dead ones.

One cannot actually see turnover happening, but some of its signs are visible. Picture an ordinary lake at the end of winter when the ice has already thinned considerably and is getting "rotten." In this condition it is not safe to walk on the ice, which has holes in it and looks somehow worm-eaten. What is happening to cause this "rot" is that small columns of air and/or water are permeating the ice, weakening it. A warm spring rain or even a significant wind can break this up quickly, piling up the remaining shards of winter ice on the shore. As shoreline waves sweep through this last icy slush, the sound is like champagne glasses breaking, a celebration of the beginning of spring. This happens very fast: The breakup of the ice, which then is washed toward the shore, often occurs in only a few hours. Only those close to the shore at the right moment can hear this "ice-out." It is the beginning of spring turnover.

In large lakes turnover occurs in various areas of the lake over several weeks. Its progress depends on how warm the days are, how turbulent the lake is, and whether the currents are weak or powerful. The latter two factors are affected by the shape of the lake's basin. Lake Baikal definitely turns over, but its lowest layers never get very warm.

SUMMER LAYERS

By the time a lake finishes turning over toward the end of the spring, heat stability returns. Three basic layers form and do not mix in summertime, except under unusual circumstances (such as a swimmer doing a cannonball or a hurricane happening). The lake becomes stratified, in other words layered.

The lowest level, called the *hypolimnion,* stays colder. The epilimnion, on top, stays warm, though it can be turbulent from wind and waves. And the *metalimnion,* which also stays in place, varies a lot in temperature from its top (warmer) to its bottom (colder). Some of these differences are evident if one "treads water" in a lake in summertime. Your feet feel colder than your shoulders.

FALL TURNOVER LEADS TO WINTER

As summer turns to autumn, colder air cools the surface. This makes the water denser. The colder, denser water sinks, allowing the less-dense water at the bottom of the lake to move up to the surface. Again, the lake "turns over." This usually happens gradually. Only a vigorous fall windstorm can power a turnover that lasts only a few hours. The whole spring process reverses itself.

During winter some heat from the winter sun does enter the lake, right through the ice. Dark ice transmits more of the solar radiation, while white ice (which includes snow and refrozen bubbles) reflects more of this weak heat back up to the atmosphere. The ice also contributes by "capping" the lake, holding in whatever heat is left.

This process occurs in all nontropical lakes that are deep enough to have water layers at different temperatures—those deeper than about 20 feet (6 m).

POLLUTION

Even with a refreshing turnover, Lake Baikal is not completely clean. The southern part, around the city of Irkutsk, is contaminated with chemicals, and more work must be done here before this city can become the popular ecotourism site it wishes to be. As of now, the unique Baikal seal, the nerpa (or yerpa), as well as area birds, are being affected.

The pollutants in this part of the lake form an array of chemicals. Effluent from the area pulp-and-paper mills, including PCBs (polychlorinated biphenyls) and other organochlorine chemicals, are significant. Two chemical plants also contribute toxic mercury to the large Angara River flowing into Baikal, an immense 2.5 tons per month of it according to one estimate. Organochlorine pesticides such as DDT are also washing into the lake from several of these sources and even blowing in from farther-away agricultural areas.

There may be more problems to come. Oil resources west of Lake Baikal, now that they will be exploited via a pipeline too close to the lake, will place its national parkland, many of its rivers, and the adjacent natural areas at risk of spills. Some of the many earthquakes in the area could easily rupture this pipeline, too, allowing oil to gush out.

The northern areas of Lake Baikal are extremely clean, however. The water pollution levels of Lake Baikal even as a whole are considerably less than, say, lakes in California.

AN OLD LAKE AND EVOLUTION

Lake Baikal's isolation has helped to keep it clean, and the situation also fosters the development of its species. Evolution here has had the chance to mold species unique to this lake. In fact Baikal has the most endemic species of any lake in the world, even more than the Caspian Sea. Out of approximately 2,500 animal species, 82 percent live nowhere else in the world. Many of the plants and microbes have not yet been studied thoroughly, but many of them may also be endemic.

Of the freshwater snails, which have been researched here, one group definitely has speciated (became a separate species) right in this lake over the eons. It often happens this way: Some members of the original species become isolated from the rest, perhaps because a mass of rock in a rifting episode moves to separate them. These creatures then breed only with the others in "their" isolated area. Over thousands up to millions of years, the two groups become so different that they will not or cannot breed with the others of their original species, even if they encountered them. They have just become too different, a different species.

To confirm the speciation of the snails, scientists isolated the genes from each group and compared them to one another and to fossilized species from the same group of creatures. But in the case of the Baikal seal, the differences are quite obvious. It has a much flatter face and bigger eyes than seals elsewhere. It also has no neck, and its rear flippers look much more like a set of fingers (with loose skin in between) than do the flippers of most seals. These back flippers flap out to help the seal steer guide its swimming.

A LAKE STUDIED INTENSIVELY

There are many international teams of geologists working here. Their methods of research include: the submersibles and temperature probes mentioned earlier; chemical analysis of the plankton in the lake, using a type of X-ray called "synchrotron radiation X-ray fluorescent analysis"; a "hydrolab" tube of electronic equipment, which, when lowered, tests, analyzes, and prints out information on the temperature, depth, acidity, salinity, and dissolved oxygen in a given area of the lake; a fluorometer that uses a laser to measure the amount of chlorophyll in the water; and many other methods.

Three additional kinds of geological research methods in the field here will be explored in more detail in the next sections: drilling cores; rock dating methods; and neutrino experiments.

IN THE FIELD: DRILLING CORES

Lake Baikal is one of the best places in the world for this kind of geological research. This ancient lake, exceptionally deep and relatively pristine, holds eons of geological history "in cold storage." The Siberian setting actually offers an advantage too: In winter scientists can drag even drastically heavy mining equipment right out on the ice—and park it there for months at a time.

Geologists require heavy equipment for drilling core samples, since they must force the hollow metal tube or box down through the water, through the sediments, and into the rock layers well below the bottom of the lake. The mining machinery then pulls the tube back up, and the geologists remove the metal "skin." The core is then carefully preserved and stored as a layered column of hardened silts and rocks. It is striped history to the trained eye.

The deeper the core drilled, generally, the farther back in history it goes. More than 100 cores from Lake Baikal are now in a "library" that reveals geological history back 10 to 12 million years. They show, among many other things, when rifting occurred here, and where and when glaciers invaded the general area.

One core, in storage, labeled BDP-98, can serve as an example. In its 1,970-foot (600-m) length, geologists can see at least 10 million years worth of layers and have looked at them to learn climate history. In some of the layers of this long core sample, *diatoms* and biogenic silica (sandy rock from the shells of sea creatures), and types of *plankton*, are especially abundant. A flowering of life like this in the lake indicates a period of warming at that time. Some such biologically rich layers date back to the *Miocene epoch* (25 to 12 million years ago) and the *Early-Middle Pliocene* (12 to 2 million years ago) here. Part of this particular core holds the oldest lake sediments ever discovered in any existing lake anywhere on the planet.

This core, and many of the others in the geologists' "library," were drilled from the Academician Ridge area of the lake. This is an isolated place where rivers do not wash in directly (and do not appear to have done so in the past) and where water turbulence is low in general. A situation like this is ideal since it kept the geological record from getting scrambled every time a large rainstorm occurred in the past (and made the rivers dump in a lot of extra sediment). Instead, the major, geologically relevant changes can be seen more clearly. One of these might be a thick layer of consistent rock that indicates an episode of rifting. Another layer, of evergreen pollen, would denote a period with a colder climate (ideal for evergreens). Another might feature high concentrations of tiny diatom skeletons; these single-celled algae are known to die in huge numbers when the water is particularly cold. Geologists can even discern from core samples which time periods had especially thick snowcover on the lake in winter; fewer organisms are found in that slice of core since few lived through those winters (less light came in through the thicker "lid").

Quite recent pulses of glaciation can be seen in various Lake Baikal cores also. One warm period has been spotted at between 127,000 and 115,000 years ago and another ending only about 4,500 years ago here. These can then be compared to climate records from elsewhere in the world to give an even bigger picture. It appears, for example, that Siberia entered one period of glaciation several thousand years before Europe did. And the Baikal area seems also to be very sensitive to changes in climate, based on changes in the amount of solar heat received. Temperatures have risen and dropped here as much as 57°F (14°C) during periods of area glaciation, a far greater swing than in most places. (For more examples of the core sampling research technique, see chapter 1: Caspian Sea, chapter 5: Lake Titicaca, chapter 6: Lake Vänern, and chapter 10: Great Slave Lake.)

IN THE FIELD: CARBON 14 ROCK DATING

Looking at the layers of a drilled core sample does not yield much insight unless and until geologists can figure out what period of history each slice came from. They do this here through three methods of dating the ages of the rock: carbon 14 dating, potassium 40-argon dating, and magnetic polarity dating. All are used at Baikal, as well as elsewhere. (Please see chapter 1: Caspian Sea and chapter 5: Lake Titicaca for more on these methods.)

Carbon 14 dating takes advantage of the fact that nitrogen in the atmosphere is continually blasted with cosmic rays, which turn it into a very mildly radioactive form of carbon, called carbon 14. The plants of the planet breathe in carbon while they are alive, and some of that remains in their tissues after they die and are, perhaps, fossilized within the sediments of a lake. All radioactive elements such as carbon 14 gradually decay, each at a different rate, and this process has been analyzed. So scientists know that half the carbon 14 in a slice of sediment decays every 5,730 years. A half of that half decays in another 5,730 years, and so on. Thus, 5,730 years is called the half-life of the carbon 14 element. This sets up the dating yardstick, and then scientists measure how much carbon 14 is in a layer of the rock core.

Alert readers will notice that, after a while, there would not be much if any carbon 14 left. And, in fact, this dating method takes scientists back only about 40,000 years before it becomes impractical to use. It also does not work at all on rock since rock was not a living plant or animal. (But materials like wood, shell, pottery, linen, and pollen can be dated using this method.) It works well for "recent" history.

IN THE FIELD: POTASSIUM ROCK DATING

The potassium 40-argon method is similarly mathematical, but the half-life of potassium 40 (the mildly radioactive version) is much longer, 1.25 billion years. If the ratio of this potassium in the rock to the argon (another element) in the rock is 1 to 1, that rock layer is probably 1.25 billion years old. And if that ratio is 3 to 1, the rock is likely to be 2.5 billion years old.

The method is appropriate for rock layers that are not necessarily fossilized plants. The radiation measured here comes not from atmosphere breathed in by living things but from forces in the seething core of the Earth. The rocks down there incorporate radioactive elements and then are cycled back up and into the crustal plates where they can be found and their constituents measured.

Rocks that have been reheated by tectonic forces nearer the surface leak argon, however, and that can mean that geologists have learned the date for that event and not older periods of that rock's history. The rock may have been reheated tectonically several times. Not all kinds of rock contain potassium and argon either, further complicating the issue. Yet this method can be quite useful, as is the carbon 14 method.

There are several other radioisotopes used in rock dating also, notably two kinds of uranium and rubidium.

IN THE FIELD: MAGNETIC POLARITY DATING

Magnetic polarity dating is quite different from the two methods above, and takes advantage of the fact that the Earth's magnetic polarity has shifted quite a few times since the planet formed. The North Magnetic Pole became the South Magnetic Pole and vice versa (though the landmasses themselves did not change position). This seemingly quite strange phenomenon occurs because of seething motions of huge rock masses deep within the Earth.

Any surface or near surface rock that is now magnetic "locked in" its magnetic polarity, matching the one that the Earth itself had at the time that rock solidified. If it remelted, it locked in that new polarity then, too. Quite a few of these polarity-reversal time periods are known. So the polarity of magnetically rich rocks (such as iron) can be "read" against this known "calendar."

Interestingly, our planet's magnetic polarity is beginning one of its shifts or flips *right now*. Scientists can see the current field weakening, which always happens at the beginning of one of these periods. The last time our polarity shifted was about 780,000 years ago. It usually takes fewer than 10,000 years for a shift to happen once it begins. This is an extremely important area of study for geologists of the near future, and, though the parameters are beyond the scope of this book, the phenomenon can be quite disruptive, even dangerous.

IN THE FIELD: NEUTRINO EXPERIMENTS

This new kind of research at Lake Baikal is also quite different from anything else discussed in the chapter. It uses the extreme depth of the lake, the massive water volume itself, as a kind of "telescope" to look for evidence of the curious cosmic particles called neutrinos. Lake Baikal was home to the first such neutrino detector in the world; now there are detectors deep in the Mediterranean, deep in an old mine shaft in Minnesota, and elsewhere.

Why look for high-energy neutrinos? It is because these visitors from distant outer space would constitute evidence of events happening elsewhere, namely inside the centers of galaxies, in binary (or two-star) pairings, in strange, short blasts of gamma ray radiation, and in other phenomena of the outer universe. These neutrinos are unusual particles, seemingly without mass, and they are as difficult to study as they are significant.

The neutrino detector at Lake Baikal lies under .7 mile (1.1 km) of water, in a deep location about 2.25 miles (3.6 km) offshore in the southern part of the lake. Nearly 200 "eyes" in the detector, grouped together, look for a special kind of quick flicker tracks called Cherenkov radiation. That indicates the fast path of a neutrino. (The amount of light reaching this depth from more local sources, such as the Sun, is mostly screened out at this depth, and the few photons of light that do descend have been measured and can be subtracted as distractions.)

Full operation of Baikal's neutrino detector began in 1998, and more than 100 neutrino events have been detected. But the experiment is still new here and elsewhere around the world. Much remains to be studied by future geologists and other scientists—an unusual use for an unusual lake.

Lake Baikal holds the freshest water of any lake on the planet. Parts of its bottom are still geologically active, and this deepest lake is continuing to deepen.

5

Lake Titicaca
Western South America

The name of this lake means Stone Puma, a puma being a mountain lion. Lake Titicaca is indeed a large creature of the mountains. Lying on a vast, high plateau between two arcs of the Andes Mountains, it is the highest lake in the world that is also deep enough to be navigable: Its elevation is just over 12,500 feet (3,812 m) above sea level.

By volume of water Lake Titicaca is the largest lake in South America and the 19th largest in the world. In extent it covers more than 3,000 square miles (8,000 km²), stretches more than 110 miles (177 km) long, lies 50 miles (80 km) across at its widest point, and reaches a maximum depth of about 1,200 feet (300 m) during the summer in a year of good rainfall.

Lake Titicaca, lying part in southern Peru and part in northern Bolivia, is also both a tropical and a desert lake. It actually remains warm enough to help heat its environment year round; its latitude, about 15°S, makes it comparable to Guatemala (about 15 degrees from the equator in the other direction). The lake loses almost as much water to evaporation each year (more than 90 percent) as it receives from its rivers and the limited rainfall; only one river flows out of Titicaca and it transports little water away. The lake receives low levels of precipitation since it lies in the *rainshadow* of the Andes. (For more on rainshadows, please see chapter 1: Caspian Sea.)

Though the vast Amazonian rain forest lies over the Andes' Eastern Mountains beyond Lake Titicaca, the lake's rainfall, scant, occurs primarily during its short December to March summer. So the lake is gradually becoming saltier. (When low levels of freshwater enter a lake, natural salts build up as they leach out from the rocks and soil.) Its overall salt level here is about .1 ounce per gallon (800 mg/l).

Lake Titicaca sits on a vast plateau called the Altiplano (or high plain), a broad, long north-south stretch of arid land between the Cordillera Oriental (the Eastern Mountains of the Andes) and the Cordillera Occidental (the Andes's Western Mountains, which include active volcanoes). The largest salt flat in the world, the Salar de Uyuni, is to its southwest. Its dry shoreline can be seen in the color insert on page C-4.

Peaks of the Andes can be seen from Lake Titicaca, and this mountain range is very active *tectonically*, resulting in frequent earthquakes at Titicaca. These "shudders" regularly damage the roads and railways the people use to get their farm products to market in the many surrounding towns. Textile manufacturing, mining, and illegal drugs such as heroin are also part of commercial activity here, with indigenous people in the area now trying to achieve more control over the oil and gas resources.

Lake Titicaca is home to more than 40 islands, two main kinds of native fish (a catfish and a smaller black-striped fish), trout (which were introduced and altered local ecology for the worse by introducing a fish parasite), and a species of frog that grows to almost one foot (.3 m) long. The lake is so high in altitude and so far from any other cool freshwater environments that its native organisms were probably introduced originally on the feathers and in the wastes of birds who flew to it. It still has relatively few fish compared to most lakes.

A narrow ridge separates the lake into two basins, though they are connected by a natural canal called the Strait of Tiquina. Only a small amount of water is exchanged between them. The larger, deeper, northwestern basin is called Lake Grande in Peru and Lake Chucuito in Bolivia and the smaller, southeastern one goes by the name of Lake Pequeno in Peru and Lake Huinaymarca in Bolivia.

TECTONIC ORIGINS

Lake Titicaca is of both glacial and tectonic origin. Since the *tectonic activity* began first chronologically, it shall be discussed first.

The activity began with the Andes. The Andes Mountains, near Titicaca (as can be seen in the color insert on page C-3) extend down virtually the entire west coast of South America. Even the Falkland Islands off the continent's southeastern tip are a continuation of this immense, high mountain range. And the Andes themselves form a partial arc of an even more extensive planetary feature, called the *Ring of Fire*. This "ring" is the tectonically active rim of the whole Pacific Ocean. It extends its "geoaction" all the way up the west coast of the United States from California up to southern Alaska, then west to Russia, south through Japan, the Philippines and Indonesia, and all the way to New Zealand. An Earth-sized geological phenomenon, the Ring of Fire is noted for its dramatic and often drastically destructive earthquakes and active volcanoes. These "fireworks," which also build up volcanic mountains around the world, are the result of clashes between the Pacific *plate* and the various other continental plates that abut it.

It is not a coincidence that the Andes are near the Peruvian coast here, or that mountains are near the coast anywhere on the Ring of Fire. The Andes of South America are a mighty uplift caused as the Pacific crustal plate collides here with the South American or Nazca plate. Part of the land gets pushed up, or uplifted, and lava also gets blasted out of volcanoes; the result is highlands, volcanic mountains, and other mountains. The geological action occurs because the land on the oceanic plate gets shoved under the continental plate and toward the *mantle* and *core* of the Earth; the phenomenon is called a *subduction zone*.

This kind of slow but steady drama has been going on in western South America for a long time already, and it will continue as far as geologists can see into the future. The Ring of Fire is not cooling down, here or anywhere. The Andes are still growing. But the process does have stages.

STAGES OF DEVELOPMENT

By the beginning of the *Mesozoic epoch* (about 250 million years ago), the land that now forms the Titicaca basin was already well above water level. This landmass included what is now South America and also all of what is now Africa. They split gradually, forcing Africa eastward and South America westward, right against the Pacific plate. By the end of the *Jurassic epoch* (about 140 million years ago), crustal folding and volcanism were intense, leading to mountain building and ocean trench building here.

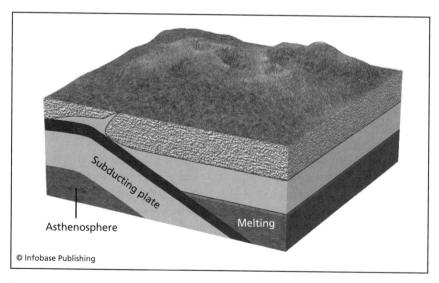

Asthenosphere   Melting

Subducting plate

© Infobase Publishing

This drawing indicates how an oceanic plate moves under a continental plate in a process called subduction. The violent force and rock melting that result have made the Andes Mountains near Lake Titicaca.

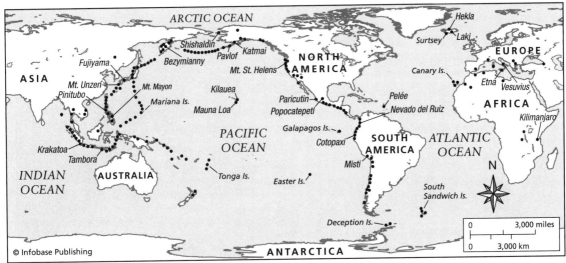

The map shows the location of the planet's major volcanoes, most of them along the Ring of Fire, a section of which lies near Lake Titicaca.

The Andes also grew on and off during the entire *Cretaceous* period (from 140 to 65 million years ago), with periods of erosion in between periods of uplift. These mountains are considered a "young" range, and are still indeed growing. In the last 10 million years alone, some areas have doubled in height. And everything we see now here is less than 40 million years old. The broad, high valley in which Titicaca began formed in this uplift, as can be seen in the color insert on page C-4.

GLACIAL ORIGIN

Though Lake Titicaca is quite close to the equator—and lakes are actually quite rare here in our planet's "Warm Belt"—there has indeed been some glaciation in the area. The last maximum pulse of glaciation was 26,000 to 14,000 years ago (especially in the 21,000 to 18,000 period) right at Lake Titicaca. (This is much longer ago than, say, at Lake Baikal or Lake Superior.)

Since that last glacial maximum, wetter and drier periods have alternated in the area. For about the last 4,000 years the Titicaca area has been in a wetter phase. Without that, it might well have evaporated completely.

The reason for glaciation this far south is the high elevation of the Andes Mountains, whose height means quite cold temperatures. Lake Titicaca's early valley basin became a valley glacier. As the land subsided between the two arcs of the Andes to make the Altiplano, the basin remained and gradually filled with meltwater.

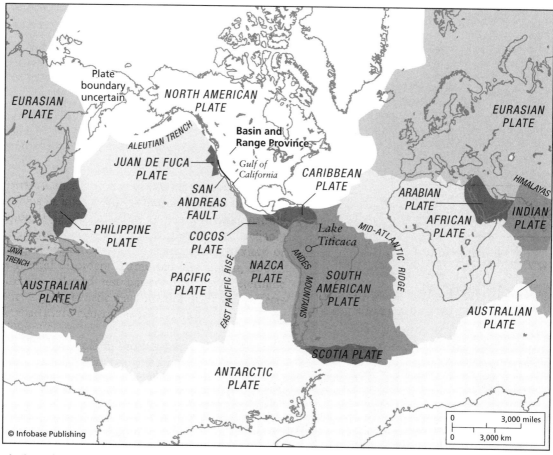

The boundaries of our planet's major plates and some of the smaller ones indicate that Lake Titicaca is very near to areas of tectonic activity.

Throughout all the pulses of glaciation over the last 2 million years, Lake Titicaca's water levels have gone up and down. It was quite low, for example, about 90,000 years ago and also between 8,000 and 3,600 years ago. These "lowstands" can be seen by geologists when they direct seismic pulses down through the *sediments* and rocks. Sedimentary material at the shore of a lake is always different from what has been under deeper water, and the seismic pulses travel differently through different materials. Lake levels, and what they show about ancient climate, are a major area of research by geologists here. We shall return to them in the "In the Field" section at the end of the chapter.

LAKE CHEMISTRY

In Lake Titicaca, a great deal of solar heat enters the lake at the surface, and the energy of the tropical Sun penetrates down deep. The heat is distributed down somewhat farther by the high desert winds (which also contribute, even more, to the evaporation rate).

The lake's mixed upper layers are high in nitrogen. It is, in these ways, a typical Warm Belt lake, though one at high elevation. Too much nitrogen in a lake provides the excess food that allows levels of algae, bacteria, and *plankton* to multiply. Nitrogen in lakes is one of the key research areas of geologists.

Nitrogen typically enters a lake several ways: in rain and snowmelt; via groundwater seepage; by the actions of various species of algae, bacteria, and plants that can "fix" or manufacture it especially in the presence of the ample sunlight here; via fertilizer runoff from agricultural operations; in human sewage and animal wastes; and even by lightning. Lightning over a lake "burns" the nitrogen out of the atmosphere itself, allowing it to fall into a lake; this usually accounts, though, for only about 1 percent of a lake's nitrogen intake. Taken together, these sources can often provide a lake with too much nitrogen, as they do here.

How the bacteria, as opposed to the algae and other plants, fix the nitrogen in a lake is an area that would benefit from more research by ge-

In this view of Lake Titicaca, women gaze at the Isla del Sol. *(www.shutterstock.com)*

ologists of the future. Nitrogen is subtracted from a lake as it is taken up by the algae and other organisms, which then deposit it in the sediments as they die. It remains down there until it is stirred up.

CLIMATE CHANGE AND LOCAL AGRICULTURE

Wetter and drier periods at Lake Titicaca have had a tremendous influence on the local civilizations here through history. (Some of the ruins along the lakeshore can be seen in the color insert on page C-4.) These changes in moisture have been analyzed by geologists in lake sediment cores by the carbon 14 dating method (see chapter 4: Lake Baikal for a discussion of this method). The beginning of a dry period, about 1,000 years ago, which lasted about 300 years, ruined local agriculture. That probably caused the Inca civilization to begin its collapse, even before the Spanish arrived with their weaponry and ambitions in the New World.

LAKE LEVELS YIELD MUCH INFORMATION

Lake Titicaca's lake levels have been studied, and are being studied, for many reasons, notably to get information on valley glaciation, on rainfall,

TROPICAL LAKES CAN EXPLODE

Though an exploding lake disaster has not occurred at Lake Titicaca, it can happen in some deep tropical lakes. The best-known examples of exploding lakes are Lake Nyos and Lake Monoun, both in Cameroon, Africa. Both lakes have crater or bowl-shaped basins (not the case at Lake Titicaca), which sets the stage for the drama.

A tropical lake in danger of exploding is one that is dense with living things, which decompose and release carbon dioxide as they die and rot. If that tropical lake has a volcanic origin, it already has additional gases on its lower levels. And if that tropical, volcanic lake is deep—Lake Nyos, for example, is 682 feet (208 m) deep—the carbon dioxide may build up on bottom layers in immense amounts. Then the lake will begin to turn over (see chapter 4: Lake Baikal for this process). But what can happen next is an immense and sudden release of carbon dioxide. In fact it can shoot up at 165 to 295 feet (50 to 90 m) per second! The effect is like opening a giant soft drink can, one the same diameter as the lake.

Carbon dioxide is a dense gas, which does not dissipate in the air above the lake. Instead, it sinks and begins to slide along the land, moving low over the whole area surrounding the lake. It quickly forms a vast, low layer of invisible gas—a gas that is fatal to mammals if breathed at air concentrations of more than about 30 percent. Breathing carbon dioxide in these significant concentrations asphyxiates all people and animals. Some 1,800 people and many more animals were killed in one such event at Lake Nyos in 1986.

Villagers described the terror to geologists who were called in to help from around the world. The event first began with a rumble, then a white mist appeared over the lake, and next came a huge roar. The entire lake quickly turned red. Only people high up in the hills escaped.

The geologists realize that they cannot stop the buildup of the carbon dioxide. But they are now installing pipes, attempting to gradually vent the carbon dioxide up from the bottom. So far it is only partially working, and danger remains.

ANCIENT LOCAL AGRICULTURE AND NITROGEN

Lake Titicaca is significant in human history, since early people have been living here for at least 5,000 years and began agriculture as early as about 1500 B.C.E. in the area. So the lake is home to one of the oldest human cultures in the Americas.

The people, known as the Inca and related groups, especially the Tiwanaku, constructed an elaborate and subtle civilization that included "raised fields" for growing their agricultural crops near the lake. Like flat terraces that stair-stepped uphill, these fields were irrigated by broad canals that the people built around the edges. The Inca culture lasted here in full force until about 1,000 years ago, then faded drastically during the 16th century, when Spanish explorers conquered the area.

Contemporary researchers have found the raised field method of agriculture to be very effective in producing good crop yields in the area, though it does allow nitrogen runoff to reach the lake in significant amounts. Near Titicaca, a few hundred families are still preserving some of the old ways.

and on salinity. Low lake levels can mean that water was tied up as ice, and high lake levels often mean glacial melting. The research also bears on the likely future of the remaining high valley glaciers in the area; these are important today for freshwater drinking and irrigation in the area.

Lake levels at Titicaca also tell geologists about atmospheric and rainfall patterns over the whole tropical Pacific and Atlantic. This kind of research also develops information about the salinity of the lake in the past and toward the future. Freshwater rain balances the buildup of salts in a lake. Too much saltiness can damage drinking water quality, fishing, and the uses of the lake for agricultural water and even hydropower.

We will discuss Lake Titicaca's lake levels in connection with each of these three factors in turn: glaciation, rainfall, and salinity. Geology is known as an "earth science" for good reason: the history of lake levels in a large lake such as Titicaca supplements and enhances other knowledge about an entire large region of the Earth.

LAKE LEVELS AND GLACIATION

Geologists have noted many changes in the level of Lake Titicaca, especially over the last 30,000 years. Though it has never been dangerously close to disappearing for lack of water, it has definitely swung 330 feet (100 m) deeper or shallower quite a few times. Most of these changes are related to the glacier and its pulses, though not always solely to them.

In glaciated periods the lake looked considerably different than it does now. In a tropical area such as this, ice covered only the highest elevations—creating the valley glaciers—and lake levels actually remained high at Titicaca for long stretches since evaporation was lower and snowfall higher. These "highstands" (high water periods) have been investigated by geologists. From 15,000 years ago to 11,000 years ago, for example, the immediate area was about 20 percent wetter and up to 41°F (5°C) colder than it is today. The lake has been discovered to have been "deep, fresh, and overflowing" in those days, far different from the high evaporation rate and the salinity we see here today. Until about 8,500 to 8,300 years ago, Titicaca was still at a considerably higher level than it is now, but with some short dips down in level. Even the highest elevation valley glaciers in the areas south of here were melting fast at the time, providing water to the lake. After that period of highstands Titicaca Lake levels began to drop.

Over the last 30,000 years "lowstands" (low water levels) have been detected, too. For example, the lowest lake levels of all occurred beginning about 6,000 years ago, and especially at about 5,300 years ago. Other low-stands have been dated at about 3,200 to 2,800 years ago, 2,400 to 2,200 years ago, 1,700 to 1,500 years ago, and 900 to 600 years ago.

Some additional highstands have been found as more recent and in between the lowstands, with especially deep levels about 3,500 years ago. In the last hundred years or so, though, the lake has not changed dramatically in its level. Geologists use all this information as pieces of the puzzle, to create a picture of glaciation worldwide. Few, if any, Earth events are as significant as glaciation for the formation of lakes (or for anything else).

LAKE LEVELS AND ATMOSPHERIC RAINFALL PATTERNS

For geologists to use Lake Titicaca lake level data to understand its much broader area, the Andes and the Altiplano, they need to study other lakes in the region, too. This has been done at seven other major lakes and 25

A LAKE UNDER A DESERT

Because of all the tectonic activity on our planet, the Earth has many kinds of rock layers underground. Some of these are very hard, others softer. Two layers of hard rock with a more spongy sandstone layer in between can trap and hold rainfall quite well. Water gradually seeps down from the surface and can form huge underground lakes, called aquifers, in the more spongy rock. These aquifers may remain there underground for many thousands of years, if undisturbed by later tectonic activity or by human activity.

Libya, a desert country in the Sahara of Africa, has discovered a vast aquifer under its desert. It is bigger than the whole country of Germany, and hundreds of yards deep. The water is actually from ice age rainfall, apparently dating from two periods, one 75,000 to 25,000 years ago and the other 10,000 to 4,500 years ago. Long buried deep, it is very clean.

The Libyans have built, and are still expanding, a vast network of underground pipes to move the aquifer water to their parched cities. Some people have called the project a "pipe dream" since it requires significant pipe repairs regularly. The water pressure keeps bursting the pipes and causes water "geysers." But the value of this resource to the desert country may be greater than even the value of its underground oil resources. This "water mine" is water that is not being replenished. Rain over the Sahara is scant and seldom. Once used, the water will be gone . . . until perhaps the next ice age.

other sites in the area. Results show that there are some significant differences between Lake Titicaca's region of the Altiplano and areas north and, especially, south of it. Since the Altiplano is so vast, the northern areas are considerably more tropical. (They are much closer to the equator.)

These broader patterns allow geologists to start correlating lake levels to rainfall. Readers who have heard of El Niños probably know that rainfall on land can change dramatically based on tropical ocean forces—they affect the atmosphere above the ocean in addition to the currents within it. Discussing El Niño is well beyond the scope of a book on lakes, but it is useful to note that tropical atmosphere "cyclones" with such names as the Intertropical Convergence Zone and the Bolivian High, as well as El Niño, drive the rainfall in this area—and always have, dropping a great deal more rain on the lake in some years than others and thus affecting lake levels.

LAKE LEVELS AND SALINITY

Any desert lake has an especial tendency to become salty. (This is discussed further in chapter 1: Caspian Sea.) Salts are always being leached out everywhere, as shoreline rocks and soils gradually erode, and even more significantly as such material pours in with the rivers from farther away. Low levels of rain (freshwater) and high levels of evaporation (which takes up more of the freshwater and leaves more of the salt), which occur here, concentrate the salt even more. This effect has been happening here for a long time.

At Lake Titicaca the low lake level periods have always meant quite high salinity levels. Geologists estimate that the lake, previously not considered saline, became so about 2,000 years ago. It has been so ever since.

IN THE FIELD: "READING" CORES

Investigating the ancient sediments of a lake can yield many different kinds of information. This is accomplished through core sampling (as is further described in chapter 1: Caspian Sea and chapter 4: Lake Baikal). "Reading" these cores is done in various ways, but they all depend on knowing that younger sediments lie over older sediments.

Just three examples are illustrative. First, if a high concentration of plankton species that tolerate salty water are found at a certain level of the geologists' core sample, but primarily or only freshwater species are found at another level, they can draw a conclusion: The lake was much more saline at the time the first of those levels was laid down in the sediments. Second, when plankton species that now live only at the deeper levels of a lake are found toward the top layer of the core, geologists can be pretty sure that more of the lake was deeper at that period—in other words there was more water in the lake, meaning that lake levels were higher. And, third, if research uncovers more aquatic plants than algae in the cores from certain areas, that area was probably at or near the ancient shoreline of the period; after all, that is where aquatic plants grow. These conclusions are all based upon the assumption that plankton, algae, and aquatic plant species do not change their "behavior" much throughout time, which is well accepted as true.

Researchers have looked at core samples from Lake Titicaca in several different ways. Sediment study typically begins here (and elsewhere) with slicing the core column in half—vertically. One vertical half is stored, still in its metal tube, in a dark refrigerator, so that the geologists can demonstrate and defend their findings to other scientists. The other, "studied," half gets destroyed as they study it.

Taking the half to be studied, the geologists then make regular horizontal slices, which are, typically, .4 inch (1 cm) apart. Each of these rock "wafers" is analyzed step by step. First, geologists examine its overall density and its carbon content (carbon indicates the past presence of living things in general). Then they look for the presence of biological silica (sandy material found in shells and so indicative of shelled creatures). They also search for various chemical isotopes (versions of the chemical)—higher strontium levels, for example, indicate that the lake was more saline at that period. They identify, too, the various species of *diatoms*. Obvious, visible fossils can also be present for analysis, though living things have often been reduced to their chemistry under the pressures that made the rock. Since whatever lived in the lake long ago was adjusted to the nature of the lake at that period, these former living things are a good key to its condition at that time.

Geologists study the concentrations of the core materials mentioned above in different ways. To measure the carbon, for example, they see how much is emitted when they burn the sample to a cinder. To measure the biological silica, they need to dissolve the sample slice in household bleach. Bleach is also used to isolate the larger, visible fossils, which then are dated using the carbon 14 technique (described in chapter 4: Lake Baikal). After cleaning, the carbon, nitrogen, and isotopes of other chemicals are studied using *mass spectrometry*. This technique, and the *seismic profiling* also done here, will be described in the "In the Field" sections of other chapters, since they are techniques commonly used to study lakes around the world in addition to Lake Titicaca.

Lake Titicaca, located in the Tropics but at very high elevations, was formed by glaciation. It is now a desert lake, the highest in the world that is deep enough for ships to traverse.

6

Lake Vänern

Northern Europe

On a map of Sweden, Lake Vänern would take a big fresh bite out of the country's middle. About 2,150 square miles (5,600 km^2) in extent, it is 87 miles long (140 km) and decorated with a large archipelago of islands called Millesvik. The lake's average depth is 88 feet (27 m), its deepest point 347 feet (106 m) down.

Vänern is the fourth largest lake in all of Europe and the largest between the Ural Mountains and the Atlantic Ocean. The 28th-largest lake in the world, it stretches across most of Sweden's east-west dimension. The lake's southern tip lies near the city of Göteborg, where Volvo cars are made for the worldwide market. Its eastern shore is just a couple of hours' drive west of Stockholm, the capital city on the opposite side of the country. And its northern shore is close to Sweden's border with Norway. About a dozen larger and smaller towns touch its edges.

This beautiful lake lies in a "lake district" rich in lakes and forests and laced with small streams and rivers. Europe's lakes lie mostly in a wide, roughly east-west, zone, many tens and tens of thousands of them in countries from Britain to Finland. Though Vänern has an ample companion lake, Vättern, most of the lakes that dot these European latitudes are smaller. We see a similar phenomenon in the United States, in the northern tier of states from Maine through Minnesota, where the Great Lakes are accompanied by many tens of thousands of smaller lakes. And Canada has a similar zone, an even larger *terrain* of lakes and forests. Why lakes are often found in districts is a geological question that this chapter shall address.

In a typical lake district resources are generally exploited along two main dimensions. The first is timber, used by the wood products and paper products industries. The second is through the creation and use of hydroelectric power, which harnesses the flow of the many rivers. More than 100 rivers here at Lake Vänern are harnessed to make electricity.

The primary reason for this blue "polka-dotting" of the planet, the creation of lake districts, is the glaciers. The glaciation will be discussed, but first, Lake Vänern's even longer ago origins will be described.

A winter scene shows the wooded shore of Lake Vänern. *(Index Stock Imagery)*

ORIGINS

Lake Vänern lies in a stable stretch of the Eurasian *plate*, one of the broad rocky slabs of the Earth's *crust* that carry the continents. The area is called the Scandinavian *shield*. (For a map of all the Earth's shields, or broad central and stable areas, see chapter 3: Lake Superior.) Shield areas are now geologically quiet, with no *tectonic activity* taking place. Because of this no one need fear an earthquake, nor admire a distant volcano, at Lake Vänern.

When one goes further back in time, however, more action was taking place. In the *Precambrian epoch* (4 billion to 600 million years ago), a period of emphatic tectonic activity occurred near here, though not at what would become Lake Vänern. Areas both north and northeast of the lake and south of it show evidence of ancient crustal collision, land deformation, mountain building and mountain erosion, thickening of the crust, and rotation and rumpling of the terrain. This happened here, not only in the Precambrian but also in the period from about 1.675 million to 975,000 years ago. This later date, well after the Precambrian epoch ended, was probably the last major reworking of the land in the area. In between these two periods, during the *Cretaceous* period (135 to 70 million years ago), the land that is now under Lake Vänern's water was once part of the ancient Tethys Sea. At this time mainland Scandinavia and Greenland were still attached.

Land-action near continental shields is defined as *orogenic activity*. Orogenic belts, also called *mobile belts* are the impact or collision zones at the edges of the stable continental sections or shields. In these belts the land is compressed, squeezed, pressed down, lifted up, folded, and thus "recycled" by tectonic activity, often in the form of ancient earthquakes and volcanoes. An orogenic phase is short in geological terms, usually lasting "only" tens of millions of years.

After that phase ended here, and the period of the Tethys Sea passed, the land that would later hold Lake Vänern settled down, looking and acting like part of the shield, as it does today. Even its narrow peninsulas, such as the one shown in the color insert on page C-5, are stable.

GLACIAL ORIGINS

Lake Vänern as we see it now is "young." Well beyond and after the original tectonic molding, the land required a glacier to make a lake. A classic glacial lake, it is a typical one across the temperate zone of the planet. Most of the lakes of the world are actually found in this zone and are anywhere from about 18,000 to about 9,000 years old. Their basins were molded into final form by the glacial ice sheet as it advanced, then filled with water as it retreated. The glacial ice in more northerly places, such as the Lake Vänern area, took longer to melt than it did farther south.

This lake is only about 9,000 years old. (As we saw in chapter 4: Lake Baikal, that lake is highly unusual in being so much older.)

The glaciers of the world, even today, are great white bulldozers. Each year they push and shove around approximately 4.3 billion tons of rock and soil. Just imagine how much scraping and crunching was done by the immense glaciers of the past as they advanced or retreated and grew heavier or lighter, depending upon local snowfall. They made tens and tens of thousands of lakes in the lake districts of the world, smaller ones from single large blobs of ice.

Near Lake Vänern, though across the border in Norway, glaciation has not entirely vanished. Valley glaciers still exist at high elevations, a few white dots too minuscule to appear on most maps. Elsewhere in Scandinavia, Iceland's Vatnajökull glacier (the largest in Europe) is still vigorous. Any summer day visitors can walk right up to one of its lobes (like a snout or paw) and see plenty of black lava rock, sand, and other *sediments* on its ice surface. This material both coats the ice and curls up in front of it, ready to be shoved forward, probably next winter. The glacier looks as though it has a dirty paw, though it is more like the edge of a giant moving van.

We still live in the Ice Age, but in a warm "interglacial" period. The last true heyday of the great ice was about 20,000 to 18,000 years ago. After that the melting became quite steady. What looks like a typical, ordinary world to us—glaciers and ice mostly at both poles—is only a planet snapshot, our one small, precious, moment of geological history.

WHY GLACIERS?

To ask why there were, and still are, glaciers is to ask why it snows. Suppose that, today, it started to snow fairly often—and all year long. The air had chilled enough that this snow never melted significantly, even in the summer. Gradually the snow would build up as the years proceeded, compressing into ice, to make a glacier. Why would it snow so incessantly? There are several reasons.

POSITION AND SHAPE OF THE CONTINENTS

At various times of Earth's history, the continents were collected together differently, and these broader continental masses were also in different positions on the globe. Looking at it as a 3-D puzzle, slide a big continental mass closer to the North Pole or South Pole. What happens? That area will receive more snow. The poles have always been colder than the rest of the planet because they receive less solar radiation. If a greater proportion of the planet's lands are closer to a pole, even a bit closer, the snow is less likely to melt there—and more likely to build a glacier.

Just as important, wherever a continental mass is positioned, the parts of it closer to the ocean are warmer and the interior areas colder.

HEYDAY OF THE GLACIERS

The period of glaciation studied most commonly by geologists is the Pleistocene, the time period beginning about 2 million years ago. This is because the evidence is far more available for research than that of the more ancient glaciations, which is buried deep down. But, as has been discussed earlier in this chapter, glaciation is caused, ultimately, by planetary cycles. These have been traced back 2.4 billion years, as can be seen from this list. Perhaps researchers of the future will be able to go back even further. There is no reason to think glaciers could not have been present earlier. White and green, green and white, the Earth has alternated in and out of glaciation.

TIME (YEARS AGO)	EVENT
2.4 billion	First major ice age
700 million	The great Precambrian ice age
250 million	The great Permian ice age
250–65 million	Interval of warm and relatively uniform climate
65 million	Climate deteriorates; poles become much colder
30 million	First major glacial episode in Antarctica
15 million	Second major glacial episode in Antarctica
4 million	Ice covers Greenland and the Arctic Ocean
3 million	First glacial episode in North America
1 million	First major interglacial
100,000	Most recent glacial episode
20,000–18,000	Last glacial maximum
15,000–10,000	Melting of ice sheets
10,000–present	Present interglacial

Most of the lakes of the world were formed primarily by glacial forces the way Lake Vänern was. Others originated partly or wholly in tectonic forces, which often placed them in mountainous areas. Both these origins create cold lakes.

Warm-water lakes are actually quite unusual. An example of one is Lake Okeechobee in Florida. It is second only to Lake Michigan in its extent, nearly 735 square miles (1,900 km²).

This is because oceans do not generally freeze—currents and waves keep the water moving, and the water is also saltier, freezing only at a lower temperature. This expanse of open water creates a warming effect on the land's coasts in the colder seasons of the year. Inland this warming ocean effect is lost. So, in the interior of any continental mass, ice builds up more easily. With the land shaped into larger continental masses in the past (remember that they had not split up), there was less coast and more interior. This increased the chances for a glacial buildup.

Another factor enhances glaciation. As some of the Earth's plates converged, especially those now holding India and southern Asia, huge mountain chains were uplifted. Not only the Himalayas in this area but the Andes in South America and the Rockies in the United States were high enough to intercept storms. This allowed much extra snow to fall onto the land (as opposed to the ocean). There it could build glaciers.

OCEAN CURRENTS AND GLACIERS

Oceans contribute the second factor that can affect glaciation. They typically have powerful, near-planetary sized, currents within them. These currents, such as the Gulf Stream, move and keep moving, primarily because of heat differences. This "heat engine" begins with water nearer the equator, which is warmer than water toward the poles.

These heat differences power a kind of invisible conveyor belt, in the past and in the present. The warmer water in the surface layers of the ocean is more buoyant than the colder water—it actually weighs less. But as the current sweeps up from the equator north toward areas such as northern Europe today, its surface layers cool. As this water cools, it sinks, and, as on an upside down conveyor belt, moves down and south again. This large-scale movement occurs in any current, even smaller, colder ones like the Labrador Current, which remains in the high north, but they are especially important in the Gulf Stream.

As the Gulf Stream moves water masses toward the North Pole in modern times, its path has been also affected by the landmasses as they exist today. The current is nudged away by Canada and Greenland, which are in its way, and so it moves around to warm the waters surrounding western Europe. The air above this warmer water also becomes warmer than air elsewhere. This is a current that has, then, changed the history of a continent. It is large enough to do so: The Gulf Stream carries 20 times as much water flow as all of Earth's rivers put together. Without the Gulf Stream and the stream of corresponding warmer air above it, Lake Vänern might never have formed when it did—the glacier might have covered Scandinavia and other northern regions for many thousands of years longer.

Temperature difference is not the only force that affects currents such as the Gulf Stream. Changes in the water's salinity or its saltiness also do. Fresher water is less dense, or lighter, than saltier water. Though most people think of the ocean as uniformly salty, it is not. In areas and times of greater evaporation—the hotter, drier condition—surface layers of the ocean become less salty as the fresher water rises. (Water evaporates easily, while salt, a heavier molecule, does so much less readily.) And, more important for the northern world, any freshwater that runs into the ocean dilutes it and therefore makes it less salty. This freshwater comes from rain, snowmelt, and the melting of glaciers. "Extra" glacial water, since it can come in immense amounts, can create major changes.

In this aerial photo taken by a NASA satellite, a dust storm covers most of the dry environs of the Caspian Sea. *(NASA/Visible Earth)*

The Aral Sea's shrinkage results in new islands appearing regularly. *(CORBIS)*

The green color indicates what is left of the Aral Sea, and the brownish areas are stretches of the former lake that have dried up. *(Courtesy of the National Aeronautics and Space Administration/ Visible Earth)*

The Palisade Head on the rocky and wooded North Shore of Lake Superior is the highest cliff on the lake. *(www.shutterstock.com)*

Lake Baikal's rocky beach meets the stormy water. *(CORBIS)*

Behind Lake Titicaca's blue waters rise the Andes Mountains. *(National Geographic Image Collection)*

One of Lake Titicaca's islands lies dry offshore. *(CORBIS)*

The ruins of an ancient Inca temple lie along Lake Titicaca. *(CORBIS)*

A long, wooded peninsula reaches out into Lake Vänern. *(Courtesy of the Land Survey of Sweden/Mats Berglund)*

A recreation area lies between the forest and Lake Vänern. *(Courtesy of the Land Survey of Sweden/Mats Berglund)*

Steep cliffs surround Crater Lake, framing a view of Wizard Island. *(www.shutterstock.com)*

An old lava formation stretches down to the lake level of Crater Lake. *(www.shutterstock.com)*

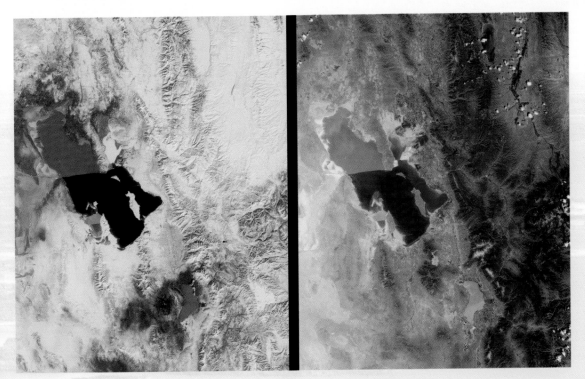

In this two-part NASA aerial the left image shows winter, when a lot of snow falls on the Wasatch Range of mountains to the east and around the Great Salt Lake, and the right-hand image is summer. *(NASA/Visible Earth)*

As far north as Great Slave Lake, vegetation grows low on the rocky shore. *(CORBIS)*

The huge nest of an eagle is high above Great Slave Lake. *(CORBIS)*

In the high north, twilight is long and the Northern Lights are already building in the sky. *(National Geographic Image Collection)*

An impressive amount of this extra freshwater is already reaching the North Atlantic right now from glaciers melting in the Arctic, and this has reduced the salinity of the Gulf Stream in the North Atlantic. The result is that the *thermohaline* circulation is changing. This could be dangerous. If the Gulf Stream were to become disrupted or rerouted—as it could be if enough glacial melting occurs—all of northern Europe could become much colder. This might be enough to begin a new period of glaciation, and quite suddenly, like throwing the wrong switch on a train's track.

The tipping point does not seem to have happened—yet. In the last 100 years world temperatures on land are warmer by 1°F (.56°C). That change may not sound like much, but the system is complex. Strangely enough, heat also has an important role in creating glaciers.

SMALL CHANGES, BIG EFFECTS

Changes in temperature can create new phases of glaciation even if they are very small. Excess *greenhouse gases* in the atmosphere, especially tiny amounts of extra carbon dioxide, could warm the Arctic enough to melt huge stretches of the glacial ice there—and relatively quickly. This is gradually beginning to happen already. How long might it be until we have taken the first step toward another ice age? Geologists estimate somewhere between a few decades and a few thousand years.

The problem is that, once the process gets going, it accelerates itself. Ice is reflective, bouncing heat (as well as light) back to the atmosphere. So less Arctic ice cover can actually cool the Earth significantly. This is one way glaciation proceeds, once it has started.

Human activity with its impacts upon carbon dioxide effluents, glacial melting, and ocean current rerouting could kick off a new glacial period. But glaciation occurred well before people walked the planet; so there is more to the story.

THE TILT OF THE EARTH

Because of the way our planet formed eons ago, the Earth is slightly tilted on its axis. This is why summer and winter are different in the Northern and Southern Hemispheres. Summer in a given location occurs when the hemisphere of that location is tilted toward the Sun, and winter occurs when it is tilted away from it. The angle is about 23.5° away from vertical and is fairly stable. But the angle does change over a cycle of about 41,000 years. This affects the amount of solar radiation received in a given hemisphere.

In addition, throughout geological history, the axis of the Earth itself also wobbles. Picture the Earth's axis as a stick pushed down at the North Pole to come out at the South Pole. The tip of that stick moves to make a little circle against the background of stars. This effect also changes the angle and amount of sunlight received. One of these invisible circles takes somewhat more than 20,000 years. These wobble circles happen because the Earth is not quite a perfect sphere—it is fatter at the equator—and the Sun's and Moon's gravitational fields, both tugging on our planet, unbalance it slightly.

The result is that our Northern Hemisphere, for example, could angle farther away from the Sun (all year long)—and for quite a few thousand years at a time. It would thereby receive less heat and experience more snow than rain. That can set the stage for glaciation. Of all the causes of glaciation, these two cycles, along with the next force—the Milankovitch Cycle—are the most significant.

MILANKOVITCH CYCLES

Our planet has another major quirk that affects glaciation. This irregularity is not in the Earth's axis, but rather in the shape of our planet's orbit around the Sun. It is not a perfect circle, but an ellipse. And it is not completely stable.

Slight variations in the annual three-dimensional path our planet takes make for small differences in the amount of solar radiation received. There is a cycle to this, too, called the Milankovitch cycle, and it occurs over about 100,000 years. If a noticeable variation happens at, say, the Northern Hemisphere's June position in the Earth's yearly travel around the Sun, and if that means less, not more, solar radiation, the Northern Hemisphere can experience a heat deficit. Just a few degrees difference—fewer than 10°F (−12°C)—can start the building of a glacier.

And additional complexity remains. The ellipse itself seems to become more elongated, in a cycle that seems to last about 400,000 years.

MORE RESEARCH NEEDED

The above four cycles—roughly 41,000 years, 20,000 to 26,000 years, 100,000 years, and 400,000 years—work either partly or wholly in tandem or in opposition at various times. Because of this, geologists of the future have their work cut out for them. But the cycles did seem to have come together about 18,000 years ago. They launched the big, though gradual, melt that eventually ended the most recent pulse of glaciation. Exit the mastodons and mammoth. Greetings, Lake Vänern and all the glacial lake districts of the world. Green forest meets blue water, as can be seen in the color insert on page C-5.

WILL THE ICE AGE CONTINUE?

As long as the Earth has the irregularities in its axis and its orbit and the present positioning of the major ocean currents and the continental masses stays fixed, the pattern of glacial pulses and interglacial warmer periods should continue. It could, however, be significantly affected by global warming caused by human activity, as mentioned above.

Other "wild cards" exist in the system, too, even seemingly insignificant factors such as dust. A massive, worldwide volcanic eruption, or a huge meteorite hit (which blasts dust and rock up into the atmosphere), or, certainly a large nuclear explosion would raise more than enough dust to significantly block the amount of solar radiation we receive.

Once a period of glaciation begins, it can present a confusing picture. Right now, most glaciers of the world are melting, but some are growing from extra snowfall. Pleistocene specialists within geology will be increasingly called upon to sort all this out and to comment upon global warming.

LAKE ACIDITY

Geologists study many kinds of contemporary changes within Lake Vänern, too. An important one is the acid level of the water. Too much acidity is fatal to fish and any other present-day, lake-dwelling creature.

Studying acidity is especially important for lakes with rocky shores in areas of former glaciers, such as Lake Vänern, since they tend to be acidic anyway. All those rocks left by the glaciers leach out calcium, magnesium, various salts, biocarbonate and carbonate, sulfates, and chlorides, which run into the lake during rains and snowmelt. These lake district lakes also receive organic acids from forest and shoreline soils. These factors alter the chemical balance of the lake's water to make it more acidic, which is the reason northern lakes often look so clear—they are too acidic for many forms of life. Geologists use their knowledge of chemistry to assess acidity levels.

Geologists are not too concerned as long as acidification happens naturally, however. But lakes such as Lake Vänern and many others are also becoming more acidic from air pollutants. Inorganic carbon, mostly as dissolved carbon dioxide, is raining down out of the atmosphere on all our lakes. It dissolves very easily in water. This chemistry gives a boost to photosynthesis, the process by which plants take in solar energy and the nutrients to live. More of these acid-making pollutants thus means more living plants—plants like pond weeds, cyanobacteria, and algae. While this acidity is more subtle than extreme, *geochemists* consider acidification a major area of study.

OXYGEN IN THE LAKE

Plants are a crucial factor in the oxygen levels of a lake, but they are not the only factor. Since a lake with plenty of dissolved oxygen is a cleaner lake, the balance, or "oxygen budget," of a lake is another important area of geological research.

Oxygen enters the lake from the atmosphere above it ("air" is about 20 percent oxygen), unless blocked near the surface by too many

POLLUTION CHALLENGES

Lakes can encounter four major kinds of overall problems: acidification, eutrophication, siltation, and pollution from toxic materials. Vänern's challenges are acidification and mercury levels (a toxic material in high enough doses). The other problems are described to provide perspective.

Eutrophication of a lake, sometimes called its "dying," happens when excessive amounts of chemicals, especially phosphorous and nitrogen, become established in the lake. These chemicals, present in large amounts in lawn and agricultural treatments, are the food for algae and other plants. The lake becomes choked with these plants, turning the water a gunky green and providing an unpleasant smell. The lake gradually fills with this excess plant life, which then drink up and crowd out the visible water entirely. Eventually all that is left is wet weeds.

Siltation, usually caused by agriculture around the lake, can also be caused by yard erosion, is the filling up of the lake basin with eroded soils. The soils are often also contaminated with pesticides. Not only does the lake fill up, but the chemistry of the soil can add mercury to the lake, too.

Toxic materials, which can enter a lake, are most commonly heavy metals, chlorinated hydrocarbons (from power plants and elsewhere), and even radioactive materials.

Lake Vänern's wildlife is not doing too badly. Some 30 species of birds breed near it, with many more migrating through. And 34 species of fish breed in the lake or the rivers that flow into it. Species not doing well here now include salmon and a variety of tern.

overgrown plants such as algae. Oxygen levels can be enhanced by turbulence, wind, currents, lake turnover, and other factors. Large amounts of oxygen are also created by plants via photosynthesis. (Plants breathe in carbon dioxide and breathe out oxygen.) This is the "plus" side of the oxygen budget.

On the "minus" side, oxygen is withdrawn from the lake by air-breathing organisms such as fish, and in chemical reactions not created by biological organisms. In lakes with not enough dissolved oxygen, such as small ponds in or near cities, most or all of the fish die over the winter. Their decomposition in spring also sucks oxygen out of the lake. The lake's bacteria use up oxygen, too, as they multiply, and then again as their bodies decay. (City and suburban lakes are usually restocked with fish each spring by park departments.)

The "oxygen budget" or metabolism of dissolved oxygen is in pretty good shape here at Lake Vänern. Forested areas around it are more natural than they are in many other places. But this lake is not escaping the air pollution from nearby and far away.

MORE LAKE CHEMISTRY

Geologists typically study other chemical cycles in lakes too. The organic carbon budget (the form of carbon found in living things as opposed to places like rocks) and the iron-manganese-sulfur profile (or balance) are just two examples. A living lake needs small amounts of many chemicals —they are not all considered pollutants by any means. But they must be balanced.

Plants, when dry, have an organic carbon content of 40 to 60 percent. When a plant dies, some of this carbon is eaten by bacteria as the plant decays. Carbon also helps to stabilize the water chemistry of the whole lake to keep it "healthy." Getting exact measures of how this is happening at different levels of the lake and at different times is a geological research area.

Iron and manganese also need to be in a good balance in a lake like Vänern. Too much iron is toxic to lake creatures, and low manganese allows algae to flourish. Evergreen forests like those around areas of the Vänern shoreline adds manganese to the lake; this happens as rainwater drains through the forest litter of pine needles and the like. The additional manganese helps keep algae levels down in Vänern.

Finding ways to kill algae naturally and safely is an area of geology research here and elsewhere. Metals such as copper and the trace element selenium are known to be bad for algae but also affect other forms of lake life. Pumping chemicals like these in by the gallon can kill the fish. And the lakes of the world are already getting excess heavy metal even beyond copper—namely radium, lead, aluminum, and other metals that can act as nutrients for plant growth. Vänern receives some cadmium and zinc in the effluent from the paper products industry on its shores. How to deal with metals in a lake requires much more attention from geologists of the future.

Sulfur is also increasingly entering Lake Vänern, and this provides another important area for geological research. Some can come in from the weathering of rocks and soil, some from volcanic gases (though this is not a factor at Vänern), and some from animal wastes. Most crucially, however, too much sulfur rains down as sulfur dioxide and sulfuric acid. These are air pollutants from the burning of fossil fuels at power plants and elsewhere.

As the sulfur dissolves in the water, most of it becomes sulfate. When plants and living creatures decay in water that is too high in sulfate, the result is hydrogen sulfide. This sulfide chemical smells almost the same as a rotten egg. (Fortunately, Lake Vänern does not experience this.) Geologists often study the sulfur cycle in a lake and attempt to improve its results.

A relatively clean lake like Vänern does not have too much iron, has a good level of manganese, and probably does not have excess sulfur. But these issues are under study.

Thinking about lake chemistry involves, then, pondering the inorganic metals and the organic life (plants, fish, and so on). Readers might think that metal particles do not interact with living things, but they sometimes do. In some cases the metallic elements are needed in very small amounts for the plants' photosynthesis (they draw them in through their pores). In other cases the bacteria in a lake actually digest the metal, transforming it into an organic form. These interactions provide complexity for geochemists.

MERCURY

Mercury may well be the best example of this relation between a metal and living things in a lake. It is definitely an issue in Lake Vänern, a problem at least equal in seriousness to acidification here. Mercury's major source as a pollutant is coal-burning power plants. It can travel on the wind many miles, then blow down onto a lake or fall down in the rainwater. Near Lake Vänern is a chloralkai plant, which, as it makes chlorine gas and sodium hydroxide for the forest industry, emits mercury, too. A form of mercury can even be created in dead leaves, which wash into the shallow areas of the lake; if they become stagnant, they are attacked by bacteria that turn the inorganic metal into an organic form. This form, dangerous to humans, is methylmercury.

The methylmercury is taken in by the fish as part of the water they absorb and the food they eat. The chemical is then concentrated many thousands of times in their flesh. The bigger and older the fish, the more mercury it accumulates. The result is that the creature at the top of the food chain, eating fish, can consume enough of this mercury to suffer brain damage. That creature is us.

Fortunately, Swedish authorities have cut mercury emissions over the last 30-plus years here at Lake Vänern. The amounts in the pike, perch, and other fish are going down, but they are not yet low enough.

OTHER POLLUTANTS

Lake Vänern also has elevated levels of phosphorous (primarily from agricultural and lawn fertilizers) and of PCPs and POPs, powerful industrial and agricultural chemicals that wash in or arrive by air from far away. This lake, however, is probably at least as clean as any lake most of us have seen. Compared to the water in, say, the Hudson River in New York City, for example, it could be considered the finest spring water.

IN THE FIELD: POLLEN COUNTING

Geologists also study lakes to learn about the climate of the past. These studies are conducted as a way to understand both the pulses of glaciation and the lives of the early people who lived around the lake. Counting pollen grains, and whatever is mixed in with them, is, actually, key detective work. This is done through core samples, the geological technique also described in chapter 1: Caspian Sea, chapter 4: Lake Baikal, chapter 5:

Lake Titicaca, and chapter 10: Great Slave Lake. Geologists pull up long cores of sediment from deep down below the lake bottom, so deep that the material has become solid layers. Each core is, in a way, like striped fossils. The layers are matched by experts to known dates.

Think about what could have fallen down into a lake and around its shores at various times throughout history, and then compacted under whatever arrived next. If geologists find a lot more pine tree pollen in a given slice of their core sample than they do apple tree pollen, they can conclude that that period had a colder climate. Is there a lot of corn and wheat pollen in one layer, but none in the layer below it? That means people had arrived to live around the lake, farming those crops. What about many pieces of old turtle shells? That would indicate that the lake was warmer and boggier during that period, a fine turtle habitat.

There are many more indicators too. A lot of soot in a prehistoric layer means forest fires (and, so, no glaciers). Lots of carbonate rock means that an ocean was here during that period, its shelled sea creatures now decayed to form that mineral. Very low levels of all kinds of pollen indicate a period of drought—the trees were having a hard time surviving and so made less pollen. Especially thick pollen-rich slices after thinner slices of low pollen counts means that summers were especially long in that period. A large amount of soil particles found in a layer indicate periods of heavy rain. Geologists with pollen cores are real detectives. And lakes like Lake Vänern are rich "crime scenes."

As Europe's largest lake, Lake Vänern is part of a lake district. Sets of lakes like these are the visible footprints of chunks of glacier, melted long ago.

❖ 7 ❖✧✧✧✧✧✧✧✧✧✧✧✧✧✧✧✧✧✧✧✧✧✧✧✧✧

Lake Eyre

Australia

Lake Eyre, in the desert Outback of Australia, is sometimes the 24th largest lake in the world—but it also sometimes does a vanishing act. "Now you see it, now you don't." Called a seasonal salt lake, it always receives some water in the rainy season from its three wild, undammed rivers—the Neales River, Cooper Creek, and the Diamantina River. Some years the runoff fills it full. In other years with lower runoff from the rivers—and only the typical few inches of rainfall here—it can be much smaller and shallower. Some years it actually disappears.

What is left when Lake Eyre vanishes is its immediate basin, called a *saltpan* when dry. This is a low area where natural salts remain in and on the soil once the heat of the desert sun has evaporated virtually all the water. No rivers are responsible for the lake's "magic act," since none drains water out. The disappearance of this desert lake, when it occurs, usually occurs over about a year.

Lake Eyre, the largest lake in the world to be able to vanish, has ranged in modern times from more than about 3,670 square miles (9,500 km²) in extent, with a shoreline of more than 130 miles (209 km) to a dry lake bed with a few water holes around it. Early in the 20th century, before 1950, Lake Eyre was considered permanently gone. But then it began to return. In 1974, 1989, and especially 2000, it transformed itself back into a major lake. The maximum depth of the lake in this period was 18.7 feet (5.7 m) in 1974.

ITS LOCATION

Lake Eyre's broad, low basin, which can be considered its most extensive possible "bowl," covers about 500,000 square miles (1,300,000 km²). This is about one-sixth the extent of the Australian continent, and about twice the size of Texas.

The "elevation" of Eyre is about 52 feet (16 m) below sea level. All drainage is in, not out, of an area so low, even lower than Death Valley in California. In dry years, however, even the incoming rivers dry up. In fact

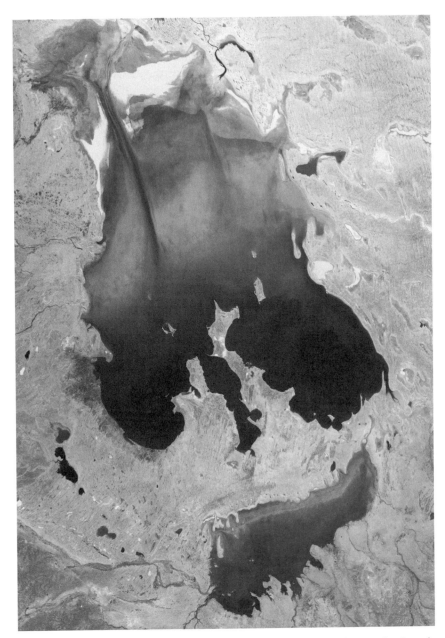

In a year with enough rainfall, such as 1984 pictured here, Lake Eyre has ample, though salty, water. The white areas are shiny, flat salt. *(Landsat 5/Government of Australia)*

this area of Australia is called Channel Country because of the beautiful and intricate dry river, creek, and stream channels laced through it, easily visible because they are empty of water. A few waterholes generally hold water even in dry periods, enabling some wildlife to survive here. In wet

---

SOIL AND WILDLIFE

Lake Eyre is very salty when its water has vanished. When a lake, large or small, evaporates, a lot is left that is not water. Here at Lake Eyre that means the minerals and other substances brought in by the rivers and by the winds as well as the residue in the soil from ancient rivers and from the period when the ocean flowed in, as Australia was separating from Antarctica. Both river runoff and ancient ocean contain natural salts. These salts come from minerals in the water, from the rocks, and from the residue of living creatures. Thousands of years of evaporation and not much rain (freshwater) have made the lake bottom sediments very salty here. In the years when the lake vanishes, that is what becomes visible—it is called a saltpan.

In this unusual environment one fish actually thrives: the desert goby. This fish, which manages to live around the southeastern rim of Lake Eyre, has adapted to a world where sometimes its water supply just about vanishes. It can find its oxygen in the air and in air bubbles over springs and in small water holes, as well as in the water the way fish normally do.

The goby also adjusts its metabolic rate (the body's idling speed) to existing conditions. It lowers its normal rate when it has to breathe air bubbles. And the goby raises its metabolism above normal as that water becomes saltier, which happens as Lake Eyre is evaporating.

Around Lake Eyre runs an unusual bird. Australia's largest flightless bird, the emu, looks sort of like an ostrich. Emus graze the ground for food, can run fast in packs, and typically travel many miles to find water. Nomadic creatures, they stay put only for nesting, trampling a place in the wild grass. The father incubates the eggs for 60 days, and the chicks travel with him for six months after that. They do not sing, but they do have deep rumbling voices.

---

years, though, and in the rainy season of most years, this lake lies amid verdant green wetlands. Lake Eyre and its environs are a national park, accessible only by four-wheel-drive vehicles.

OUTBACK LOCATION

The Outback of Australia is known for its dryness, and the Lake Eyre area is the driest place within it. Eyre and its broad basin sit south-central on the Australian continent. To its north is the Simpson Desert with many smaller low, dry saltpans. And to the northeast is the Great Artesian Basin, an area that tends to be dry on the surface but has water pools deep beneath the surface called aquifers. To the northwest of Lake Eyre lies even more desert. The main way that an inhospitable area like this is used is for raising sheep. Australia has about 165 million sheep, raised mostly in "sheep stations" (like ranches) in the Outback.

Only one town, Marree, is anywhere near Lake Eyre, and it has fewer than 10,000 inhabitants. In addition to sheep ranching, the general environs has some mining and oil and gas industries. Tourism is also increasing. Native people called the Maori live in this area, engaging in all these activities.

Only one town of any significant size, Alice Springs, exists anywhere in the Outback, and it is not near Lake Eyre. Australia's major cities are all on its coasts, far from this lake.

STABLE GEOLOGY NOW

Lake Eyre's geological home is a large area of Australia close to the middle of the vast Indo-Australian *plate*. This stable area, free of earthquakes, volcanoes, rifting, and other kinds of *tectonic activity*, is called a *craton* or *shield*. (See chapter 3: Lake Superior for a map of the other shields of the planet.) More than half of Australia is actually ancient shield.

Stable for a long time, the bedrock in the Lake Eyre area is about 600 million years old with some of the rocks here dating back even to 1.5 billion years ago. South of here rocks generally even older, commonly 700 to 900 million years old, hold the fossils of very ancient jellyfish and forms of algae. Near Australia's western edge some of the rocks are up to 3.65 billion years old, as old as anything ever found on Earth.

During the *Permian* period at Lake Eyre, the most recent part of the *Paleozoic epoch* of 280 to 225 million years ago, a glacier came and went in part of Lake Eyre's "neighborhood." It covered even Tasmania, the island off Australia's southeastern coast. And here, during the *Triassic* part of the *Mesozoic* (225 to 170 million years ago), mountains formed in the area; they have now eroded. This was also about the time that the oil deposits formed, though the largest of these deposits are off Australia's east coast rather than here.

A LOT OF ACTION BEFORE

Before the present period of geological calm at Lake Eyre, there was plenty of action. For a long time Australia was connected with Antarctica as a single continent. Between 590 and 540 million years ago, the land that is now in the southwest "corner" of Australia swiveled into a partial split, let some sea in, and then squeezed the sediments up into mountains. (They have now eroded into high hills).

By the *Jurassic epoch* (170 to 135 million years ago) the whole immense landmass had reached pretty much its present location. But the Australia section of it continued to pull north, as though trying to escape an icy embrace.

By about 100 million years ago, the split between Antarctica and Australia had allowed the ocean to flow in and was widening. This is what deposited the sandstone and chalk rocks in the interior, such as the giant, famous Ayers Rock (called Uluru by the Maori).

The final separation of Australia from Antarctica occurred in a prolonged blast of tectonic activity about 60 to 50 million years ago. What

Plenty of water laps at this Lake Eyre peninsula, at least in this year. *(Image Library of Australia)*

is left of that action now is a line of high mountains along the east coast and curving to the southeast, called the Australian Alps. Think of them as the stitched-up suture line of the huge "wound" that split the two continents apart.

GLACIATION

Even though Australia was, and is, much closer to the equator than Antarctica, it has had glaciers in "modern times." During the Pleistocene glaciers were common, at least at higher elevations. Australia's southern areas were ice-covered as recently as about 18,000 years ago. This period was both preceded and followed by times of rich, ancient woodlands. The trees vanished only about 5,000 years ago, probably largely burned for fuel by the ancient people. What is left from this Pleistocene period here will be discussed in the next sections.

The days of the ice are now over. Australia no longer has glaciers and is less than 10 percent forested; about half of that is rain forest on and near its equatorial north coast. And this continent is going to stay where it is for a long while. There is only one truly tectonically active area now, a single *hot spot* in the continent's southeast corner. This kind of geological feature, which elsewhere punched up the Hawaiian Islands out of the Pacific and built Iceland out of the North Atlantic floor, is a plume of upwelling lava from deep within the Earth. It is a kind of underground faucet, turned on often.

ANCIENT LAKE LEVELS

Geologists are detectives, looking for clues in the Earth. And a study of a lake's levels, part of what is called its *hydrology*, is an important focus of their detective work around the world. (It even extends to other planets.)

Here at Lake Eyre hydrology clues range from ancient beach ridges and rock debris in valleys to the eggshells of the ancient emu birds. Analysis of information like this yields evidence that, for example, Lake Eyre's maximum historical depth was once probably 82 to 89 feet (25 to 27 m); this is much deeper than in the "contemporary" times of the last few thousand years. Ancient hydrology here will be followed by information on contemporary hydrology in the "In the Field" section of the chapter.

This lake has proved to be an excellent site for relating lake water levels to ancient climate shifts in Australia and in the area's whole Indian Ocean and Pacific Ocean location. That information then provides a good-sized puzzle piece in geologists' efforts to reconstruct the pattern of the whole planet's ancient climate.

Evidence of ancient lake levels visible here seems to begin in the Late *Paleocene* (about 65 million years ago), when the land subsided to make the lake's basin. This happened as the Australian Alps were building to the east. That *orogenic* process pushed the land up in that direction, causing it to slump here.

Between then and the Pleistocene, sediments were laid down in three main phases. The first was layers of sand, silt, clay, and carbonated rock. Within this, geologists can find decayed evidence of an ancient rain forest. It lasted until the Middle *Eocene* (about 50 million years ago).

Next were deposited layers of dolomite and more clay and sand rich in magnesium. This happened in a period, which extended from late in the *Oligocene* to early in the *Miocene* (about 30 to 20 million years ago). Gradually over this period the forest and woodlands changed from thick rain forest to more scattered large patches fed by water during highly rainy, or *monsoon*, conditions.

The third period of sedimentation was characterized by a lot of red clay, sand, and silt. It washed in by river and blew in by wind during the Pleistocene. This indicates that a semiarid climate had taken hold, which then gave way to the pulses of glaciation.

ICE AGE LAKE LEVELS

Evidence in and around Lake Eyre of what was going on during the Pleistocene period here is more extensive than for the earlier periods. After all, this era began "only" about 2 million years ago. Geologists have developed regular "snapshots" of the life of the lake. With more research a whole mural can be discerned.

About 170,000 years ago, for example, the bottom of Lake Eyre, or its deepest point, was farther to the east and the lake was quite high, at least in the Neales River delta on the south side of the lake. The rivers had been flooding in because of heavy monsoons. These are drenching rains, and they create what is called the "rainy season" in the Tropics (northern Australia is in the Tropics).

A second high lake level in the Neales River area occurred about 100,000 years ago, and more than once between 130,000 and 90,000 years ago around the lake. At this time all the main river deltas—both on the monsoon-affected north side and elsewhere—were high, though the Neales River entered the lake about 12 miles (20 km) west of where it does now.

Between about 60,000 and 50,000 years ago, lake levels sank. Geologists can see, and place dates on, the high ridges that were left high and dry. They are the former beaches, seen because ancient mollusk shells and shorebird eggs are buried within them. During this period the broad Lake Eyre basin took the general shape, size, and position that it has today.

Between 65,000 and 45,000 years ago, or over the same general period as above, the lake was also wildly wet. Best estimates are that some periods within this time stretch were the most active monsoon periods in the whole Lake Eyre record. This picture has been established partly by finding evidence of the kind of grasses that grow well under monsoon rain conditions. And evidence of those grasses was found partly by chemical analysis of the fossil eggshells of the emu. What these large flightless birds eat appears chemically in their shells a few days later. Their egg-laying season is known to be from July through September, allowing a glimpse at the large proportion of seasonal grasses that had been transformed into eggshells. This kind of geological analysis is considered reliable because the feeding behavior of birds and other animals does not change much over the years.

A next identifiable stage in the life of Lake Eyre's northern side was between 50,000 and 31,000 years ago. The lake fell again during this period, establishing one more piece of the visual puzzle.

The ups and downs in lake level during the Pleistocene are a good guide to when the glacier dominated and when it melted. Ice locks up lake water, and melting raises its level. Between 33,000 or 30,000 years ago and also 17,000 or 12,000 years ago, there was both an extremely dry

THE OPPOSITE: A VERY YOUNG WET LAKE

Close to the opposite of Lake Eyre, whose terrain is very old and dry, is Lake Okeechobee in Florida. This Everglades area lake is young and wet, much like a huge wetland with cattails and other aquatic grasses. It never vanishes suddenly.

Okeechobee, once a natural link between the Kissimmee River and the Everglades, is now only about nine feet (2.7 m) deep. It has ridges—old lake shores—that date back much earlier, but the Everglades themselves have been here for only 4,000 to 6,000 years. Before that almost all of Florida was underwater, part of the ocean itself. So this lake is almost an infant.

period and an extremely wet one. Evidence of the latter has been found in layers of sand and a claylike silt that were laid down during a phase of wetlands here. Most geologists have found this particular time period especially hard to figure out, however. More work needs to be done. Lake Eyre appears to have established its modern alternation of wet and dry by about 4,000 to 3,000 years ago. And the glaciers have gone, at least for now.

RECENT GEOLOGY

Geologists can see recent evidence, from only about 150 years ago, of the arrival of the European settlers with their domestic sheep and rabbits. These animals caused the extinction of some smaller native animals. The new species ate different grasses, and so the change in species affected the kinds of grasses that were able to leave their significant fossil evidence in the soil.

CLIMATE CLUE: DUST

Arid desert now, the Lake Eyre basin creates salty dust when it shrinks. (See the sidebar on Owens Lake in chapter 1: Caspian Sea and chapter 2: Aral Sea for more on dry lake beds.) But this area has also been the recipient of millions of tons of airborne dust from elsewhere in Australia and beyond (geologists can trace it in the soil and figure out where it came from). Since this very dry incoming load is always less during periods when the monsoon rains are strong over the Indo-Pacific area, dust layers can be used to help figure out early climate swings toward dryness in the Lake Eyre basin.

During stages when Australia had glacial ice, ice never covered the whole country. It was mostly in the south. From the more tropical north, storms would sweep in, leaving layers of dust. They can be found, in thicker or thinner layers, between the layers of ice. This helps to date the periods of glaciation here.

Dust can also be studied by geologists to analyze wind patterns. If a dust layer is richer in quartz than clay, for example, that helps in figuring out where it came from and hence the prevailing winds. Winds bend the climate significantly in Australia since its north coast is so much hotter than its south.

IN THE FIELD: HYDROLOGY AFTER A FLOOD

For almost 50 years now, Lake Eyre and its basin have been studied at the actual time of flooding. The flood of 1989–90 has been researched by a team of scientists from a dozen of Australia's universities and research institutes. One part of the team used ground and aerial surveys to estimate that between 500,000 and 1 million birds moved in when the lake rose.

Hydrologists, who study water flow, even stood in Lake Eyre's incoming rivers for parts of 30 days with their instruments, this time after the flood of 2000. Clay particles in the river clogged and dried out their skin. In the process the geologists learned how water flow patterns sustain the wetlands around Lake Eyre. Floods can encourage the various fish and 45 species of waterbirds there to breed in April (not their usual season), when the water levels are high. And they are working on a computer model that will be able to predict river flow under a variety of rainfall conditions. Once complete, it will predict how long it takes for flood water in the changeable Lake Eyre to subside.

Lake Eyre, in Australia's desert or Outback, is unusual in that it ranges from one of the largest lakes in the world to almost nothing. When it is at its least extensive, wetlands around it do remain.

Crater Lake

Oregon, United States

The deepest lake in the United States, at about 1,800 feet (600 m), Crater Lake is a splash of sapphire blue high in the mountains of Oregon. It lies in a *caldera*, or the bowl-shaped crater of a volcano, in this case Mount Mazama.

Created in an eruption between 7,700 and 6,000 years ago—one that blasted the top 4,000 to 5,000 feet (1,220 to 1,524 m) off its mountain and sent out 12 cubic miles (50 km^3) of hot lava—the lake seems peaceful now. Nearly round with steep rock walls and about six miles (9.6 km) across, it can all be seen in its entirety from anywhere on the 1,000-foot (305-m) high cliffs surrounding it. Part of the dramatic scene is its small wooded island, Wizard Island, which formed in a smaller "burp" of lava about 300 years after the main eruption. Hidden under the lake's surface are two more "not-quite islands," too small to be visible above its clear surface. The smallest of these formed in an eruption only about 5,000 years ago.

Crater Lake is in the Cascade Mountains, a line of peaks that slice mostly north to south through Washington State and Oregon. All of them are high and cold—Mount Mazama and its Crater Lake receive up to 50 feet (15.25 m) of snow every winter. The Cascades divide the coastal areas to the west from the Columbia Basin to the east. And their *rain-shadow* keeps eastern Oregon a desert.

The coastal parts of Oregon and Washington State, along with those of California and Alaska, are part of the *tectonically active Ring of Fire*. They feature regular earthquakes as part of the Pacific *plate* shoves past and under the North American plate. The Cascades formed as part of this activity and were at the coast when they emerged. In fact, about 20 million years ago they were about 170 miles (275 km) northwest of where they are now. Since then, more land has been shoved up and erupted out. That has added the territory, which is now west of the mountains, and swung some of the land at an angle, like a door opening on its hinge.

The Cascades are still volcanic. Mt. Rainier, near Seattle in Washington State and not far from here, last erupted in 1850. Mt. St. Helens let loose its most recent blast in 1980, an event so loud that it could be heard about 200 miles (320 km) away. Then, after a quiet period, it was rumbling again in 2005. Mt. Hood, overlooking Portland, Oregon, and Mt. Baker are also major Cascade peaks.

Mount Mazama no longer has its pinnacle crown—that was what exploded away—but it is still an active volcano. Geologists have found hot water and steam vents on Crater Lake's bottom, a sure sign of active "plumbing." No one knows when the next eruption will happen, and the volcano is considered *dormant* now.

Crater Lake rocks are both old and new. Geologists have dated its oldest ones at about 400,000 years old (well before the eruption that created Crater Lake) and its newest at about 5,000 years old (those most "recently" burped and oozed out from the lake's bottom).

ROCK FEATURES

There are some dramatic rock features at Crater Lake, too. One, called the Devil's Backbone, arching up one of the steep walls surrounding the lake, looks like a thick dark vertical line in the surrounding rock face. It is called a *dike*, an old rock fracture that filled with lava that later hardened. The rock on both sides of this formation, not recent lava, is lighter in color than the solid vertical "backbone." This is clearly visible evidence of the eruption here.

Another area, featuring sharp pinnacles of rock emerging from solid, wavy "walls," is also the volcano's footprint. This structure was created as the last gasps of steam from the volcanic ash shot upward like vents or steam pipes. The gassy ash solidified in those upward thrusts. Since then erosion of some of the softer material has made the remaining spikes stand out much more.

Quiet, at least for now, Crater Lake is a national park and has been since 1902. Visitors can circle the lake on the 33-mile (53-km) Rim Drive to absorb the geology and the beauty of the lake. It is easy to see the lake from vantage points, such as the one shown in the color insert on page C-6. There are also many trails radiating out from it with additional high viewpoints over the water and other sites.

THE ERUPTION

The volcanic eruption that led to Crater Lake was actually the most violent anywhere on Earth in the last 10,000 years. The blast was 10 times more powerful than the famous Krakatau eruption in the Pacific in 1883, and 100 times greater than the massive Mt. St. Helens explosion nearby in 1980. Avalanches of fiery red molten rock poured out from the crown of the mountain. *Pyroclastic flows* raced out and reached a distance of 30 miles (48 km) from Mount Mazama, burning everything in their path to cinders. Lava exploded and flowed out to cover thousands of square miles. The "grey snow" of the volcanic ash sifted down for weeks afterward. It ended by covering a great stretch of land, 500,000 square miles (1,294,994 km²). Anything that escaped the volcanic forest fires probably starved to death as this choking ash blanketed the region. What on Earth could have led to this?

MOST ANCIENT ORIGINS

Once the early Pacific Ocean receded from what is now the area of Crater Lake, the *rifting* began here. From about 1.4 billion years ago to about .85 billion years ago, the land began splitting in places. *Plate tectonics* was remodeling what would be the coasts of Washington, Oregon, and California.

By the early *Paleozoic*, about 500 million years ago, two broad strips of land, extending inland from Alaska down to Mexico, lay adjacent to each other, roughly parallel to the coast. The eastern or inland strip had formerly been the edge of North America, now shoved east as the oceanic *plate* continued its pushing against the continental plate. The western strip included even more volcanic material, but the Cascade volcanic mountains had not yet formed at this stage.

By the *Mesozoic epoch* significant areas of Oregon began to experience volcanic activity. Vast areas of solid lava underground have been found and dated to this time. Land was piling up in what would be the Crater Lake area by 225 to 200 million years ago.

THE OCEAN FLOODS IN

In the early *Jurassic epoch* (about 170 million years ago) the Pacific Ocean flooded over the land, covering this area with shallow water. Geologists call it the Sundance Sea. What is now the Crater Lake region was either just underwater or just at the edge of two of the large areas of higher land. The seas receded, only to reappear in the late *Cretaceous* (about 80 to 70 million years ago). And mountains began to form again, thanks to the plate tectonics that continued to shove up land.

THE "RECENT" ERA

Fast-forwarding to "only" 40 million years ago, what would be today's Cascade Mountains began to be born. Again the cause was the collision of the crustal plates and the molten rock that results in underground clashes like these. As that eased, the mountains eroded a bit with time, but the high plateau continued to swell gradually, thanks to immense, but slower, floods of lava. The uplift then picked up its pace, and between 10 million and 3.5 million years ago, volcanic eruptions built the Cascade Range. By the end of that period the range looked roughly sim-

This shows both the cliffs and a steep island in Crater Lake. *(Klamath County Museum, Klamath Falls, Oregon)*

ilar to today's formation. Mount Mazama and the other specific peaks we see now, however, had not yet formed.

That formation finally began to happen about 400,000 years ago. Cracks developed in the *crust* and up through them began to flow lava, which hardened. As more and more such flows followed, the mountains were built up. Geologists can see some of this ancient lava in the formation on the south side of Crater Lake. Glaciers and erosion gradually wore down the mountains, too, but because of the lava flows they continued to swell overall.

Not all lava reached the surface, however. Huge lakes of molten rock remained underground then, and they do today. This is the raw material for new eruptions to come, now in storage. Pressure from underneath, from plumes of heat seething within the *mantle* of the planet, forces masses of lava to the surface at irregular intervals. That is what causes eruptions.

By 50,000 years ago Mount Mazama had fully formed. Smaller eruptions continued until about 28,000 years ago. Then everything quieted down—for a while.

CRATER LAKE'S BIRTH

The massive new eruption that was to form Crater Lake began with a false start. About 200 years before the major event, vents or cracks opened up on Mount Mazama's north side. Blasts built up what is now called Llao Rock, a mass of lava about 1,200 feet (365 m) thick.

Then came the real action. Geologists think the eruption took only a few weeks. Deafening noise, smoke, ash, dust, boulders as big as houses, all filled the air. Then, in a roar, the mountain just blew its top. Its crown vanished. Rock collapsed inward to fill the cavity, like the wound from a giant cannonball, hitting from above then bouncing out.

Gradually the lava cooled. The hardened lava made a plug in the plumbing, like a drain cap in the bottom of a fountain. The lava settled and hardened further to cement the bowl, the caldera.

This basin, not yet Crater Lake, gradually received rain and much melting snow. It took about 300 years for the caldera to fill even halfway up. During that period Wizard Island rose in two stages, from smaller eruptions. As the rains and snowmelts continued, Crater Lake finally reached its current dramatic depth and astounding beauty.

WATER CLARITY

Crater Lake's beauty comes not only from its high-mountain wilderness "apron" and steep cliffs (shown in the color insert on page C-6) but also from the clarity of its water. The lake is such an intense, luminous blue that most visitors' first remark is about its color. No rivers or streams flow in, which means that no pebbles, sand, soil, plant material, or anything else enters it this way. So there is very little particulate matter suspended in the water; this is what ordinarily scatters the sunlight and dulls the color of a lake. Here the sunlight, unscattered and unclouded, can fill the water almost to a glow. One percent of the incoming light can be seen even at the level of 263 to 328 feet (80 to 100 m) deep, which is extraordinary for any body of water. The lake's deep blue can be seen in the color photo insert on page C-6.

Crater Lake is so blue because it is so clear. Formed without the input of rivers, other lakes, or the ocean, it is relatively low in living things (which always absorb some light). Clear water absorbs the redder and yellower colors within sunlight and allows the bluer colors to be scattered upward for us to see.

A simple but important measure of water clarity, taken by park officials and by geologists here, is done with a *Secchi disk*. A simple white

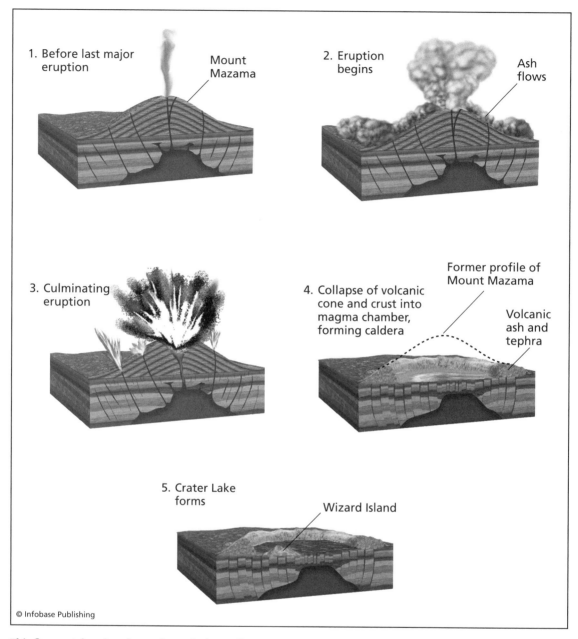

1. Before last major eruption

Mount Mazama

2. Eruption begins

Ash flows

3. Culminating eruption

4. Collapse of volcanic cone and crust into magma chamber, forming caldera

Former profile of Mount Mazama

Volcanic ash and tephra

5. Crater Lake forms

Wizard Island

© Infobase Publishing

This five-part drawing shows the explosion, collapse, and final formation that created Crater Lake.

plastic circle attached at its center to a thin rope, the disk is lowered deeper and deeper until the observer can no longer see it. Since the rope is marked like a yardstick, observers can easily note exactly how far down the disk remains visible. In the past a Secchi disk eight inches

(20 cm) in diameter could typically still be seen 100 to 130 feet (30 to 40 m) down.

Recently, with increased human activity, the Secchi numbers reached about 65 feet (20 m), much worse. A sewage leak was discovered and finally cleaned up for good. Water clarity is back up to about 130 feet (40 m). This is amazingly clear.

Microscopic plants do live in Crater Lake, though not in large enough concentrations to cloud the water. About 160 species (taxa) of *phytoplankton* have been found, different ones living in each of the three tiers of lake depth, but there are few of them compared to other lakes. Near the shore of Wizard Island and elsewhere grow some aquatic plants such as water buttercup, bitter cress, and algae moss. And there is one "benthic" or deep-water moss in the lake.

Water creatures are also quite rare here. There seem to be only about 13 species of microscopic animals in the lake, several of which migrate up and down between day and night. Fish were introduced into the lake in 1888 by park officials, namely various trout and salmon species. Unlike many such ecological "projects," this one seems to have done no real harm, since there was little biological activity to disrupt.

WATER BUDGET

Snowfall, an average of 43 feet (13 m) a winter, sifts into Crater Lake now. Snowmelt also pours in over its surrounding cliffs. But about 80 percent of the water entering Crater Lake comes in as precipitation (as opposed to runoff or seepage), and far more of that is snow than rainfall. Water is lost to the lake through evaporation (30 to 50 percent) and through seepage out (50 to 70 percent); the latter process is always present in lakes even though their bottoms appear completely solid.

Crater Lake's water budget is fairly stable, with levels remaining within 16 feet (5 m) of one another over the last 100 years or so. A given water molecule spends about 150 years in Crater Lake as its "residence time," also a mark of stability.

WATER CHEMISTRY

Since Crater Lake is so clear, geologists know that it must be both phosphorous-deficient and nitrogen-deficient, and they have verified this. More phosphorous and nitrogen would mean more algae, for one thing. These deficiencies are fine as they indicate that the sewage has been cleaned up, too.

But geologists do think that some nitrogen is upwelling from the hot water and steam vent area deep down on the lake's bottom. This upwelling helps to mix the lake's water layers, though minimally. The active thermal vents also boost the sulfate and chloride levels to a relatively high

OTHER "CRATER LAKES"

Since there are other calderas in other volcanoes around the world, and many have also filled with rainwater and snowmelt to create lakes, there are indeed other crater lakes. Australia has an entry, called Crater Lakes National Park, which features a pair of volcanic lakes, Eacham and Barrine. They are between 3 million and 20,000 years old and lie in the rain forest of northern Australia.

New Zealand also has a crater lake, called Lake Taupo, which has gotten beyond the bounds of ordinary behavior; it has burst through its own rim. A flood of about five cubic miles (20 km³) of water once took only a few weeks to spread gooey wet volcanic ash 55 feet (17 m) thick around the Taupo volcano. The lake, when it lies inside its caldera, is 240 square miles (616 sq km²) in area and formed in an eruption about 1,800 years ago. Apparently a similar flood here, but three times larger in water volume, occurred about 26,500 years ago.

Much closer to Oregon's Crater Lake are the two crater lakes of the Newberry Volcano. Its 1,000-foot (305-m)-deep caldera holds two lakes, Paulina and East Lake, and lies only about 70 miles (112 km) southwest of Crater Lake. A shield volcano, it is more of a high splat of ground than a steep mountain—"only" 8,000 feet (2,438 m) high at its summit—but still a very beautiful area. Formed by many successive lava flows, Newberry Volcano is layered like a stack of pancakes. It also features evergreen forests, wildflower meadows, and a thick lava flow only 1,300 years old. That makes the Newberry Volcano the youngest volcano in the lower 48 states.

The largest crater lake in the world is found in northern Sumatra, the Toba Caldera. This lake's longest side stretches almost 60 miles (100 km) and within it lies Samosir, an island 250 square miles (650 km²) in area.

level here. Crater Lake is quite alkaline, too; this is the opposite of acid, which means that its water can neutralize acid rain.

LAKE TEMPERATURE

Crater Lake's temperature is also taken regularly. It maintains an even temperature of about 39°F (4°C), over its long winter (October–May). The lake turns over or stratifies beginning in June. (See chapter 4: Lake Baikal for more on lake stratification.) By August surface water can reach 65°F (18°C). Below 130 feet (40 m) down, however, the "warmth" almost never goes above 40°F (5°C). It is very rare for Crater Lake to freeze over. Only in 1898, 1924, and 1949 did an ice layer form that was two to 12 inches (5 to 30 cm) thick for as long as three months.

Crater Lake has been studied intensively in many dimensions only since the mid-1980s. Before that, a rubber dinghy, Secchi disks, and not much else constituted the research equipment. A *submersible* came into use here starting in the late 1980s. By 1995 a small field lab with beds was installed in a cabin on Wizard Island for wintertime research. And a 30-foot- (9-m-) long research ship equipped with a full laboratory, is stationed here for warm weather studies.

IN THE FIELD: LAKE STUDY BY SUBMERSIBLE

A submersible is a tiny submarine or "pod" equipped to withstand the heavy weight of all the water above it (as it descends to the depths) and to provide plenty of the oxygen and technology necessary for geological research. This is an excellent, though expensive, research tool.

Over two summers featuring 50 dives, geologists used the vessel to discover the hot water and steam vents on Crater Lake's bottom. They then studied such dimensions as the "salinity gradients" of the water—the way the water's saltiness diminishes as one gets farther away from the vents. (Water sizzling up through layers of rock has acquired natural salts.) It is a very subtle difference to discover since this lake's salinity is very low. Another example of their focus was the unusual bacteria at the bottom vents. These microbes live not by the energy of sunlight (as surface creatures do), but by feeding on the chemical constituents of the steaming vents.

IN THE FIELD: LAKE DEPTHS BY SOUNDING

This research method, also called *echo sounding*, uses sound waves to determine the depth of various parts of a lake or other body of water. A transmitter directs a blast of sound straight down, and a receiver listens for it to return. Since the speed of sound through various substances is known—in the ocean it is 4,921.25 feet (1,499.9 m) per second and in lakes it is somewhat less—geologists can figure out how far down the sound went, or, in other words, the depth of the water at that location.

Sound waves bounce off other things besides the bottom, of course. At Crater Lake geologists have used a "multi-beam" sonar device attached to a research ship on the surface. It is called multi-beam because it sends many sound waves down at once, almost like a sprinkler spraying sound instead of water. Doing the whole lake in detail required 30 million soundings! A computer then analyzed the results and provided a map of the whole lake bottom.

This large project, completed in 2000, established a new and precise maximum depth for the lake—1,958 feet (596.8 m)—that year. It has enabled other scientists to find and analyze some of the huge boulders ejected by Mount Mazama as it erupted and to estimate the date when the lava solidified to form the lake's basin. The research has also pointed out landslides, tiny bottom vents, and other underwater features now being studied to learn more about the volcanic event that created this caldera lake.

Crater Lake formed in the caldera of a volcano, as that bowl-shaped depression gradually filled with water. Since it has no incoming rivers, it is low on plant and animal life, retaining its amazing clarity.

9

Great Salt Lake

Utah, United States

A shallow lake so salty that swimmers can easily float with parts of their arms and legs held up above the water, the Great Salt Lake lies west and north of the Wasatch Mountains in central Utah. To its south/southwest is desert, part of a region called the Great Basin, a 300-mile- (483-km-) wide lowland. Salt Lake City, the capital of Utah, is adjacent.

Listed as the 34th largest lake in the world, and about the size of Rhode Island, the Great Salt Lake expands and shrinks often, depending upon runoff from the mountains and the small amount of local precipitation. Its size averages 1,600 square miles (4,145 km²), though over the last 50 years alone it has ranged from 970 square miles (2,512 km²) up to 2,300 square miles (5,957 km²). It is 75 miles (121 km) in length, and 13 to 25 feet (6 to 8 m) at maximum depth.

Around the lake's edges are cracked mud, white salt flats, and plants with names like brittle greasewood. In it live plenty of half-inch-long brine shrimp and enough salt-tolerant bacteria and algae to turn the lake pink, especially in its northern section. No fish can live here, except at the mouths where rivers flow in. The water is also hard on boats. The predominant smells are dust and salt.

As inhospitable to life as the Great Salt Lake seems, its ecosystem does include wetlands in springtime, fed by runoff from the Wasatch Mountains. These provide a stopping place for more than 100 million birds, in about 250 species, on their way to Alaska for the summer.

The Great Salt Lake is known as a *pluvial* lake. That means it has no outflow by river and experiences significant increased in depth due to precipitation. It receives incoming water from several rivers, the Bear and the Jordan being two of them. Evaporation rates are very high here since the desert sun is hot.

The lake is divided into two sections by a road, with little mixing between the two. The south arm, into which all the (freshwater) rivers enter, can drop to as low as 4 percent saline. The northern arm usually

This antique image, created about 100 years ago, shows swimmers in the Great Salt Lake with Antelope Island in the background, much the same as today. *(Library of Congress, Prints & Photographs Division, Detroit Publishing Company)*

remains 26 to 28 percent salt. These two areas can differ quite a bit, especially when melted snow and rain enter the lake, as can be seen in the color insert on page C-7.

ONCE LARGER

The Great Salt Lake is the main remnant of a huge pluvial lake called Lake Bonneville. Once extending at least 20,000 square miles (51,800 km²) and reaching to a depth of 984 feet (300 m) in places, it formerly covered most of Utah, eastern Nevada, and southern Idaho. Now known instead as the Bonneville Salt Flats, this land, once underwater, blankets the area around the Great Salt Lake in hard, dry, salty land, flatter than any pancake. Some mining is done here of sodium chloride, one form of salt, along with magnesium and other minerals.

The Lake Bonneville area was fresh and wet during the warmer period of the *Pleistocene*, when the glaciers far to the north melted. Evidence of old wetlands and rivers from 11,000 to 8,800 years ago has been dis-

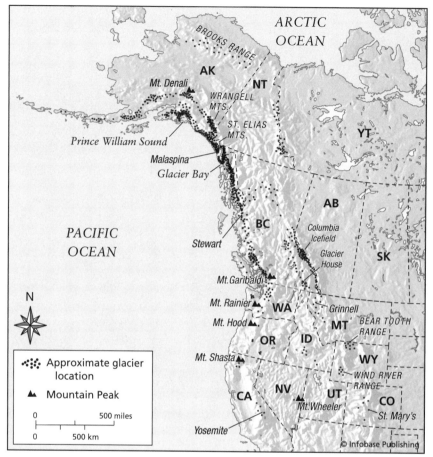

This close-up map shows where glaciers remain today in the western United States and Canada. Global warming is, however, steadily reducing their extent.

covered by geologists. This ranges from gravel beds, to the pollens of pine trees, to the fossilized "middens" (trash piles) of wood rats. As recently as between 3,400 and 1,200 years ago, the Great Salt Lake was much less salty and much deeper.

WHY A BASIN?

The Great Salt Lake lies in a basin, called the Great Basin, which is very low because the mountains around it are high. This may sound obvious, but there is more to it than what appears.

The Wasatch Mountains nearby, the Sierra Nevada in California, and the Rocky Mountains in general are places where the Earth's crust has been shoved up along *fault lines*. Plumes of *magma*, turbulent within the *crust* and *mantle* of the planet, are the engines for mountain building. As the crust rose in one area, it thinned and slumped between the new mountains. That slumping has made the low basin here.

The Earth's crust is spreading apart in this area at the rate of one inch (2.54 cm) per year. About 15 million years ago, for example, the lands that now are Salt Lake City and Reno, Nevada, were 200 to 300 miles (320 to 485 km) closer together. Over time, this stretching weakened areas of the crust enough that upwelling of lava and volcanic eruptions intruded and brought additional rock masses.

The crustal upwarping along fault lines is the process that created all the stretches of the Rocky Mountains here in the West. (Mountains of the western United States have local names, such as the Wasatch Range and the Sierra Nevada, even though many are the result of the same *orogeny*). Running roughly northwest to southeast in the United States from Washington State to Arizona, the Rockies began to form in the *Cretaceous* (135 to 70 million years ago). Though erosion has acted, the faults have regularly caused more huge blocks of crust to slip, rotate, and tilt up, adding to the height of the Rockies. Their formation became complete during the *Paleocene* (70 to 60 million years ago).

As the faulting raised rock masses, the other, lower areas became closed off into more than 140 basins, of which the Great Salt Lake's Great Basin is the largest. If you fly across the West, coming from the East or Midwest, you can see some of these isolated "pocket" basins in the mountains. Often filled with water, at least seasonally, they look whitish from salt. Many of them, though to a lesser extent than the Great Salt Lake, are saline lakes.

SALTY LAKES, DRYLAND FEATURES

From the Canadian prairies of Saskatchewan south to North Dakota and then southwest to Mono Lake and Death Valley in California are found many salty, temporary lakes. Present only in spring and summer when snowmelt floods low areas, heavy in surface salt, they are usually only a couple of feet deep. Their saltiness comes from all the salt left behind in the soil by many years of annual evaporation.

In Nevada is a distant cousin to the Great Salt Lake. Pyramid Lake is the remnant of ancient Lake Lahontan, just as Great Salt Lake is the vestige of Lake Bonneville. Lahontan was another inland sea formed well south of the immense melting glaciers to its north.

Unlike the Great Salt Lake, Pyramid Lake is deep, about 350 feet (107 m). And its lake life is quite unusual. Swimming around is a fish called the cui-ui, which dates back 2 million years, to the early Pleistocene. It has probably been here since the first glacial meltwater.

On land a distinctive dryland feature of the desert west is the hoodoo. Hoodoos are pillars, spires, and towers of rock, often very oddly balanced. A large rock may be perched on top of a thin neck of rock beneath, for example, like an odd, rocky mushroom. Many are knee-high up to a couple of stories high, but they can range more widely in size. These strange rock structures, which look as though built by an impossible magician, form in several stages. First came ancient volcanic rock (common in the West), which cracked as it cooled. Then rain, runoff, and wind have sculpted the rock, removing less dense material to achieve the hoodoo's individual shape.

WHY SALTY?

The Great Salt Lake is so salty because of its longtime desert environment and its rivers. The hot desert sun causes the freshwater to evaporate readily, leaving the salts to become concentrated. Salts are a natural element in rocks and soils and enter Great Salt Lake with its rivers. The result: a lake that is between three and eight times saltier than the ocean.

A SALT LAKE HABITAT

The Great Salt Lake is now so salty—and so isolated—that it has few living things within it. Permanent ones are a single species of brine fly, an insect called the water boatman (which lives only in the fresher water areas near the incoming rivers), two species of brine shrimp, about 23 species of algae and *diatoms*, and salt-tolerant bacteria. The brine fly larvae are eaten in massive numbers by the shorebirds migrating through Utah, flying from the Arctic to Central America.

Though it may seem surprising, the brine shrimp have been studied quite extensively by scientists. The reason is that they anchor a $10 million annual industry for fishermen in the area, and the harvest here represents about 90 percent of the world catch of brine shrimp. They are sold as food for aquarium fish.

WATER CHEMISTRY

Geologists have studied the brine shrimp as part of the Great Salt Lake's water chemistry. One thing discovered is the amount of arsenic these creatures can tolerate (arsenic, a form of salt called sodium arsenate, is definitely present in this lake). Across their whole life cycle (about three weeks), these tiny shrimp can live with an average of as much as 151 milligrams per gallon (11 mg/l) of dissolved arsenic, even more than is typically present here.

Another brine shrimp study turns up something perhaps even odder. They will, when hungry, eat the discarded parts of their own skeletons. They shed these pieces as they grow larger, and small amounts of algae and bacteria attach to the old bone bits as they float down. Brine shrimp love algae most of all, but by July each year they have eaten most of it here. This leaves them with only their "cannibalistic" algae-edged meals. (While the next generation of brine shrimp is hatching, the lake's algae have time to rebound.)

A third group of scientists has studied the effects of four lake chemicals on the growth of the algae and bacteria: ammonia, nitrate, glutamic acid, and urea. The first three help to produce *algae blooms* and the fourth benefits the bacteria. They also note that salinity in the north (saltier) arm of the lake reaches 40 to 48 ounces per gallon (300 to 360 g/l).

IN THE FIELD: SEISMIC PROFILING

This geological technique is like making a fake earthquake. A real earthquake, caused by immense force of rock masses shifting suddenly, creates three kinds of underground waves (similar to the way a loud sound creates sound waves). The first type, called P-waves, travel underground at about three to nine miles (5 to 15 km) per second, their force conveyed similar to the way a "slinky" toy changes position. The second kind, the S-waves, are a bit slower, at 2.5 to four miles (4 to 7 km) per second. These move differently: Picture a hook tied to the end of a rope, dangle it down, and then shake the other end of the rope to see this kind of force pass through the rope. The third kind, surface waves, move through surface layers of the planet—these are the waves that topple buildings and bridges in earthquakes. Taken together, these seismic waves ring the Earth like a bell, either penetrating or circling the whole planet. They can be mapped as they do so.

Geologists can create the third kind, the surface waves, by digging a hole and blasting dynamite into it. The waves thus created change speed according to what they go through—how rigid, how dense, how compressible the rock is in that area.

Here at Great Salt Lake they have used seismic blasting to map the faults in the rock under the lake. And since they already know the dates of the various rock layers, they have "seen" three major crustal movements—a total of about 40 feet (12 m)—of rock mass shifting over the last 13,500 years alone.

Great Salt Lake, an unusual lake, is shallow and so salty that few living things can survive here year round. Its salinity is enough to make swimmers quite buoyant.

Great Slave Lake

Canada

At this subarctic lake in Canada's Northwest Territories, the last glacier is news from practically yesterday. Great Slave Lake emerged from its vast white "lid" fewer than 11,000 years ago and took its present shape thousands of years after that. An observer can tell by the lake's shape which way the glacier moved; the lake is elongated in that northeast/southwest direction.

Great Slave Lake lies in the vast northern wilderness between the Mackenzie Mountains to its west and Hudson Bay to its east. Around it the *terrain* is primarily tundra, treeless Arctic plains, with some areas of dwarfed evergreens. Most of the soil remains frozen all year long; in this condition called *permafrost*, only the top few inches thaw in the summer.

The lake's shore is home to the town of Yellowknife, the province's capital, with fewer than 20,000 inhabitants. The area is part of the Canadian *shield*, ancient land now *tectonically* quiet, where the melting and reforming of rock in ancient mountain-building events have concentrated metals underground, creating more than 1,000 gold mines in the area and both coal and diamonds not far away.

The 11th largest lake in the world, Great Slave Lake covers 11,170 square miles (28,930 km^2) and reaches a significant maximum depth of 2,015 feet (614 m). The shoreline, 298 miles (480 km) long, can be seen (in part) in the color insert on page C-7.

ORIGINS

As part of the Canadian shield, the land here is very old. In fact the oldest rocks on the entire Earth, 4.03 billion years old, have been found in this area. They are ancient lavas and sediments once laid down in shallow water, proving that the planet's history began even before that. Rocks nearly this old, 3.7 to 3.4 billion years old have been found in Greenland, Minnesota, Michigan, Swaziland, and Australia. And the very oldest material—not rock masses but tiny zircon crystals—have also been found in Australia.

GLACIAL FEATURES: KETTLE LAKES, PINGO LAKES, GLACIAL POTHOLES

Kettle lakes, which get their name because many of them are rounded like the bottoms of teakettles, were created by pieces of leftover glacier. As lobes or "paws" of the glacier began to melt, often there were especially huge ice chunks within them. Many of these had become coated especially thickly with rocks and other "clothing" that blocked the sun from reaching the ice. These chunks then took longer to melt.

The large glacial chunks were also heavier. Their weight compressed the ground under them even more than the rest of the glacial lobe did. Over the several hundred years it might take one of these extra "dirty ice cubes" to melt, the bottom layer of pebbles and soil that every glacier carries with it settled into the depression in the ground. That made the lake bed. Then the melting ice gradually filled up the hollow with water.

These kettle lakes are quite common in the northern world. Both Minnesota and Wisconsin have more than 15,000 kettle lakes apiece. (The Minnesota license plate, which mentions 10,000 lakes, is not even counting most of these small ones.) Many more even than this number of kettles, if once no bigger than about 10 miles (16 km) across, already have filled in with cattails and sediments, and then solid soil. They do not look like lakes anymore. All the subarctic and Arctic regions also are home to many thousands of these kettle lakes.

Much smaller, pingo lakes form in the craters of small, cone-shaped hills across the Arctic. The hills form as water rises up through cracks in the permafrost and pushes surface soils and vegetation up into a mound. When the top of this surface material collapses back down, and the ice in the top layer of the permafrost melts in summer, a small pingo lake develops.

Glacial potholes are geological formations that look as though a giant had grabbed a kitchen scrubbie, then scraped out bowl-shaped or trough-shaped depressions right in the solid rock. These potholes are usually a few inches up to a few feet across and about twice as deep as they are wide.

The scouring is actually done by glacial rivers. Floods today do not match the force that rivers once mustered as they filled with glaciers' worth of meltwater. Any river or stream always has eddies, the sweeps and circles within the turbulent water. It was mighty eddies in glacial rivers, thick with pebbles and stones, that scoured out glacial potholes. Some of these stones, worn into spherical shapes, can still be found in place, at the bottom of the potholes—as though they were waiting for the next blast of glacial meltwater to start them whirling again at their task.

The coal found in the Great Slave Lake area formed during the *Miocene* (25 to 12 million years ago) as *sediments* settled and compressed. Evidence of an ancient continent here, about 2.5 billion years ago, in under investigation. The most "recent" tectonic activity north of the lake has been dated at about 1.7 billion years ago. The extreme depth of the lake is due to the Fort Hay *fault* under it—the water fills this deep crack in the ground. The Earth has been pretty quiet here, though, for a long time.

The *Pleistocene* (2 million years to modern times) was the Great Slave Lake area's heyday. In the period 11,800 to 8,300 years ago, for example, the lake was part of Glacial Lake McConnell, an immense body of water 92,665 square miles (240,000 km²) at its maximum extent. Even the present Great Bear Lake, another major glacial lake in the area but far to the north, was part of that glacial artifact. Floods of glacial meltwater rerouted rivers and sometimes raced along for 30 straight months during the Pleistocene. (Northern rivers generally freeze in winter.) Worldwide, more than 9.6 million cubic miles (40 million km³) of snow and ice covered about a third of the world's land during the glacier's time, and Great Slave Lake was part of that scenario.

As the ice gradually receded, Great Slave Lake's ancient animals began to arrive: giant short-faced bears (twice the weight of a grizzly bear), mastodons, sabre-toothed cats, wooly mammoths (the largest weighed in at six tons), steppe bison, white antelopes—and even the American camel, cheetah, and lion (25 percent bigger than African lions today). Left from this cast of characters today are the caribou, musk ox, Dall's sheep, pronghorn antelope, eagles (as can be seen in the color insert on page C-8) —and human beings. People, too, evolved during the Pleistocene.

DEPTH AND REBOUND

Great Slave Lake is deep not only because of the fault mentioned above. The weight of the glacier itself compressed its basin, shoving soil and rock deep into lower rock and depressing the crust. Here glaciation pushed the land down 650 to 985 feet (200 to 300 m) deeper. The glacier also scooped out the land as it moved, like a slow white river scouring and flowing downhill, when colder temperatures led the ice to thicken, strengthen, and advance.

The news today carries quite a bit about what happens to ocean levels as glaciers disappear: The glacial meltwater flows in, and the seas rise. Sea level now is at least 245 feet (75 m) higher than during the time of maximum glaciation; so this process has already been happening for a long time.

But what happens to land compressed by the glacier, as the ice vanishes between the periods of glaciation? Perhaps amazingly, the land also rises and bounces back, in something like a sigh of relief. The process is called *isostatic rebound*.

This rebound is not at all old news across the subarctic and Arctic of the world. The Great Slave Lake region is still bouncing back. Today, too, citizens of Hofn in southeast Iceland, are watching the land around their harbor rebound, and they do not like it. The rising land is closing off parts of their harbor's mouth, making it harder for their fishing fleet to motor in and out. The Icelanders can also see the rest of the glacier in question, the Vatnajökull, still immense and just a few miles away. It is an important part of their tourism industry, and they would like to see it stay, continuing as such an impressive site and keeping the land compressed.

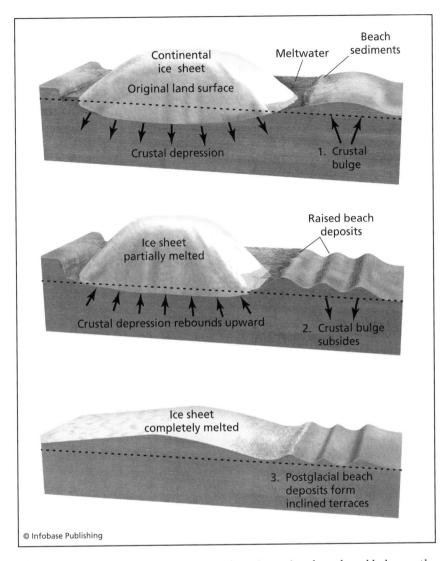

In this three-part drawing, one can see how isostatic rebound could change the location of beaches.

It is a vast understatement to say that no one can stop isostatic rebound. It is a planetary phenomenon, which, in its most recent phase of activity, has been going on for 8,000 to 10,000 years, even here in the high north. The typical rate at these latitudes is down to less than a couple of centimeters per year. At Lake Vänern (chapter 6), farther south, the rebound has dropped down to about one-10th of an inch (.254 cm) per year, and in Lake Huron and Lake Ontario it has finally ended completely.

THE NEXT GLACIER?

When the ice advances out of the Arctic the next time, the polar lands of the planet will be the first to compress again under its weight. Best estimates are that glaciation will be at its next maximum about 80,000 years from now, with a long and increasing chill leading up to that for tens of thousands of years. Will global warming affect this scenario? If so, by how much? Scientists think that the warming will not significantly slow the march of the ice, but the geologists of the future have an exceptionally important research area to address here. One thing is certain: The Earth is still in the Pleistocene. (For more on this subject, see chapter 6: Lake Vänern.) The high Arctic environment of Great Slave Lake at night can be seen in the color insert on page C-8.

ARCTIC FEATURES

Scientists studying a little-known area of ocean floor between northeast Greenland and Siberia, along a 600-mile (965-km) stretch called the Gakkel Ridge, recently found a surprise. At this *mid-ocean ridge,* which is spreading at the rate of just one quarter-inch (.635 cm) or so in both directions every year, they found volcanic domes a mile (1.6 km) high and evidence of *hydrothermal vents.* Elsewhere in the world vents like these are home to unusual life-forms such as giant tube worms. The spreading rate here is only about one-seventh the speed of other mid-ocean ridges studied, and geologists had not thought it would be possible to create these features with this velocity of spread.

Research under the ice is not simple. The geologists' equipment for this project included: ice-breaking ships (one borrowed from the Coast Guard); long, thick cables to drop their instruments down to test the water temperature and water chemistry; and dredges to shove bottom rock away.

To find out exactly what might live down there at these vents, a new kind of reinforced *submersible* must be developed. That is under way now. The depth to the bottom here is about three miles (4.82 km).

Another Arctic feature, this one common, is called "patterned ground." This geologic feature—ground that looks like the puzzle-pieced back of a turtle or an irregularly tiled floor—is found here and there across Arctic *tundra,* the subarctic, and even high mountain areas farther south. Huge fields of patterned ground can occur in the middle of nowhere, looking as though constructed by crazy giants.

The full name for the phenomenon is "sorted patterned ground," and "unsorted patterned ground." In both cases each element of the pattern is usually about four inches to three or four feet (10 cm to 1 m) across. The cause lies in the regular freezing and thawing of the top levels of the ground above, the permafrost so common in the high north. The formation of an area of patterned ground takes hundreds of years.

Over these years, once part of the process, called "frost heave," forces soil and rocks above the ground's surface with the expansion of water molecules as they freeze. This applies to both the sorted and the unsorted patterns. To create sorted patterns, in which the soils and the rocks have separated, more is required. A key factor seems to be the shape of the ice patches just underground as the freezing occurs. When they are lens-shaped, the soils slide to the edges more easily than the rocks do. And, gradually, gravity and more frost heave continues to "sort" the elements by their level of coarseness. After decades the finer soils lie in the middle of each area, the pebbles and rocks around the edges. Then the soils in the middle "slump" more as they settle, making the rocky edges look even more distinct. A polygon shape often results; this is actually a very common shape in nature and not just on turtles' backs.

IN THE FIELD: ICE CORES

One of the ways geologists study glaciation is through ice cores, excavated by drilling into the ice similar to the way core sampling is done in rock. (This latter subject is also treated in chapter 1: Caspian Sea, chapter 4: Lake Baikal, chapter 5: Lake Titicaca, and chapter 6: Lake Vänern.) The site of the most ambitious ice coring in the world is the Greenland ice pack, where 250,000 years' worth of layered ice and bedrock have been pulled up. Analyzing one of these long cores is like looking at a (long) library book.

Cores up to a couple of miles long from Greenland have provided some unusual findings on worldwide glaciation. When glaciers are advancing, the air swirls with much more dust than it does today, probably because more storms are set off as the colder air collides with the warmer air masses. When glaciers rule, there is less carbon dioxide, a *greenhouse gas* in the atmosphere; this was discovered by analyzing tiny air bubbles within the ice layers. And, at least at one point, temperatures rose so dramatically—in just 10 years—that it was like Chicago's weather turning into Atlanta's. Global warming could indeed occur that fast, though it usually takes hundreds up to thousands of years.

IN THE FIELD: MASS SPECTROMETRY

This common geological research technique has been used at Great Slave Lake to analyze the tectonic events from about 1.7 billion years ago. Geologists do this with a *mass spectrometer* in the lab, bombarding pieces of rock with a stream of electrons in a sealed chamber. Various kinds of atoms in the rock can then be weighed electrically. And this tells researchers what kinds of material are present in the original rock and how old they are.

Great Slave Lake is an impressive vestige of the most recent pulse of glaciation. Since the ice melted only a few thousand years ago, lifting that immense weight, the land itself is still bouncing back.

Conclusion

Lakes

Readers of this book have, ideally, enjoyed its unusual lakes and their superlative qualities. The largest lake in the world, though not on any of the typical lists (since it is saltwater), is the Caspian Sea. The lake that constitutes the worst ecological disaster is the Aral Sea. The "sweetwater sea" lake that covers the largest swatch of the planet in blue is Lake Superior. The lake half as old as the dinosaurs and getting deeper every year is Lake Baikal. The highest major lake is Lake Titicaca. The large European lake, found in a lake district footprint of the glacier, is Lake Vänern. The lake that waxes immense one year but can be entirely gone a few years later is Lake Eyre. The lake formed in a massive volcanic explosion is Crater Lake. The American lake so salty that is it hard to sink when swimming is the Great Salt Lake. And the high northern lake whose surrounding land is still literally rising today, now that the weight of the glacier has gone, is Great Slave Lake.

The lakes of our planet all come and go, always changing, though usually on the near-infinite time scale of geology. A volcano somewhere, erupting and collapsing at its crown, can make a new lake. A glacier can place a lake in silent, cold storage for many thousands of years. The vast processes of plate tectonics open and close lakes, even oceans. (This will continue until the heat source in the core of our planet has gone cool, as it already has on the Moon.) Global warming can evaporate lakes and pollution can poison them. All these Earth-events, and more, can happen and probably will. Those who seek to understand them, geologists, and those who like to learn about their work, will never be bored, never stop wondering why, how, and when.

The ways geologists do research has great variety. There is still plenty of work to be done with only hiking boots, a small hammer, and an educated mind. Mapping, from land, from a submersible, from a satellite, all is eliciting more attention and detailed knowledge. Mathematical models are becoming more possible—and popular—to construct as explanations for geological processes. Physical modeling in the lab offers many opportunities, too, as equipment can squeeze rock to simulate the very core of the Earth or reconstitute the surface of another planet or moon. Major experimental apparatus—from electron microscopes to mile-deep drills, from gas chromatography to mass spectrometry, and much more—analyzes rock. There is no end to what remains to be discovered and understood on our unquiet Earth.

Lakes are based, ultimately, on the nature of water. It happens to be not only common but also one of the strangest substances on Earth. Virtually every other liquid contracts as it moves toward freezing; yet water expands. Most other liquids, when "supercooled" to below 0°F (–18°C), yet remain liquid, lose their ability to absorb heat; but water soaks up heat at a great rate instead, and also becomes more compressible. (Supercooled water is found in rain clouds.) This behavior of the water molecule makes ice, in a sense, aggressive and makes clouds behave differently, both important for the lives of lakes.

Since lake water is indeed studied at this level, as well as many others, it is possible to see that many kinds of scientists are involved in research that bears on lakes: geochemists, geophysicists, paleogeologists, economic geologists, and more.

Ideally, this book has engendered deep curiosity in readers, whether to become geologists of some kind, or to become science writers, or to form part of the educated public on matters scientific. This kind of curiosity can lead readers to love our planet even more.

Glossary

algae blooms   relatively sudden, large growths of algae in a body of water, often from excess phosphorous

breccias   rocks with easily visible angular fragments, sometimes but not always formed when a meteorite hits surface rock

caldera   bowl-shaped depression at the top of a volcanic cone, formed when the volcano's summit collapses inward after an eruption

Cambrian   period of geological history from about 500 to 460 million years ago when the oceans covered much more of the world than they do today

Carboniferous   period of geological history from about 350 to 270 million years ago when the early Appalachians, early Alps, and early Himalayas began to form

Cenozoic   epoch of geological history from about 70 million years ago through today, when TECTONIC ACTIVITY and seafloor spreading were vigorous; includes the PALEOCENE, EOCENE, OLIGOCENE, MIOCENE, PLIOCENE, and PLEISTOCENE eras

core   deepest and densest part of the Earth, includes the liquid outer core and the 1,800 mile (2,900 km) down solid inner core, both primarily made of pure metal

craton   oldest, most geologically stable section of each major continent, where earthquakes and other TECTONIC ACTIVITY have not occurred for a long time, also called SHIELD

Cretaceous   period of geological history from about 135 to 70 million years ago when dinosaurs ruled, both South America/Africa and Australia/Antarctica separated, and the Rocky Mountains began to form

crust   outermost layer of the Earth which varies from 12.5 miles (20 km) to 45 miles (70 km) thick depending upon location on the planet

Devonian   period of geological history from about 400 to 350 million years ago when sea creatures ruled and the first land animals evolved along with the land vegetation

diatoms   microscopic algae that possesses a siliceous cell wall; they can accumulate as sediment

dike   narrow, tabular strip of rock, usually highly tilted or even vertical, intruded within another body of rock, often but not always solidified lava from a volcanic eruption

dormant   characteristic of a volcano which has not erupted for a long time but is not dead

echo sounding   geological research technique in which sound waves are directed at the bottom of a lake or other body of water, to analyze the depth and the nature of the bottom rock by the way sound waves return to the apparatus

endemic   life-form found in only one place, having evolved uniquely to conditions there

Eocene   period of geological history from about 60 to 40 million years ago, during which the climate of the world ended its warm period

epilimnion   top layer of a lake or other body of water

eutrophication   process by which a body of water becomes more crowded with algae and other water plants, loses many other species, and gradually dies as a viable ecosystem

faults, faulting   cracks or fractures in rock which show that the two adjacent sections have moved relative to each other

gas chromatography   process of analyzing a geological material by vaporizing it and moving it across a detector with a flow of gas

geochemistry   branch of geology which uses primarily chemistry in its research

geophysics   branch of geology which uses primarily physics in its research

glacial potholes   hollowed-out areas in solid rock, made by the force of glacial meltwater rivers and the water and pebbles they carry

glacial till   rocky soil layer deposited by a former glacier (can be many yards thick), also called "overburden"

graben   large fault that forms a valley or trough and sometimes becomes the basin of a lake

greenhouse gas   atmospheric gas, such as carbon dioxide or methane, which traps heat within our atmosphere

Holocene   period of Earth history from about 10,000 years ago to the present, when major new glaciation has halted; this period is often included as part of the PLEISTOCENE instead.

hot spot   area where the Earth's *crust* is thinner, allowing plumes of hot MAGMA to force through, creating surface volcanoes and the land they make

hydrology   the study of the movement of water in the atmosphere, land, water, and mantle of the planet

hydrothermal vents   crack or fissures on the bottom of a body of water out of which comes warm water or steam, generated through TECTONIC processes

hypolimnion   lowest layer of water in a lake or other body of water

isostatic rebound   the bouncing back of an area of Earth's CRUST after its depression by a heavy object such as a glacier

Jurassic   period of geological history from about 170 to 135 million years ago when volcanic activity was intense in the western United States, the Atlantic Ocean formed, and the continents moved close to their present positions on the Earth's surface

lacustrine   growing in a lake or pond

limnology   study of lakes and rivers which draws on geology, chemistry, and biology

lithosphere   solid top layer of the Earth's surface (including the CRUST and the outermost part of the MANTLE), about 62 miles (100 km) thick

littoral, littoral zone   top layers of a body of water where the aquatic plants grow

magma   liquid, underground lava which can flow to the surface

mantle   layer of the Earth between the CRUST and the CORE, composed of relatively dense rock

mass spectrometry   lab device in which a beam of electrons in a vacuum chamber is shot at a substance to be analyzed; computer programs then compare it to known substances and determine what it is (can be used even on tiny amounts of rock to tell what is in them)

Mesozoic Era   period of Earth's history from about 225 to 65 million years ago (includes the TRIASSIC, JURASSIC, and CRETACEOUS periods)

metalimnion   middle layer of a lake or other body of water; a zone of rapid temperature change

mid-ocean ridges   areas of the ocean where the seafloor is spreading as MAGMA wells up, can be thousands of miles long

Miocene   period of geological history from about 25 to 12 million years ago when the Alps and Himalayas reached close to their present heights and the Appalachians and Rockies were in a period of erosion

mobile belts   the TECTONICALLY active areas around the CRATON or SHIELD areas of a continent

monsoon   heavy seasonal rains characteristic of tropical and subtropical regions

moraine   massive deposit of GLACIAL TILL found at the forward edge of a glacier's former position

nuclear magnetic resonance   a type of MASS SPECTROMETRY in which radio waves are directed at a material held within a magnetic field; done to detect substances within a material by how they "sound" in these waves

Oligocene   period of geological history from about 40 to 25 million years ago, when the Alps and Himalayas continued to grow and change and when FAULTING was common in the American West

Ordovician   period of geological history from about 500 to 460 million years ago when the ocean were more extensive than today and sea creatures were the predominant life form; the same dates are used for the CAMBRIAN period.

orogenic activity   the processes involved in mountain formation

Paleocene   period of geological history from about 70 to 60 million years ago when the formation of the Rocky Mountains was largely completed and the landscape of the planet took on close to its present form

paleogeology   branch of geology which specializes in the most ancient parts of geological history

Paleozoic   epoch of geological history from about 500 to 225 million years ago; includes the CAMBRIAN, ORDOVICIAN, SILURIAN, DEVONIAN, CARBONIFEROUS, and PERMIAN

Pangaea   the supercontinent, composed of the land of all present continents; began to break up about 200 million years ago

pelagic   pertaining to the ocean

permafrost   soil permanently frozen, found in Arctic and subarctic regions

Permian   period of geological history from about 270 to 225 million years ago, when icecaps were extensive in the southern hemisphere

phytoplankton   tiniest plants and bacteria in a body of water, which move primarily with water turbulence

plankton   algae and other small plants that live in bodies of water

plastic   flowing or moldable rock

plate   large, rigid piece of the Earth's CRUST which moves across the mantle's surface because of seafloor spreading at the MID-OCEAN RIDGES; plate interactions are the main force in the development of mountains, volcanoes, earthquakes, continental changes, even oceans; currently geologists consider there to be seven major plates, eight medium ones, and about 20 smaller ones

plate tectonics   the study of the TECTONIC ACTIVITY of the Earth's PLATES

Pleistocene, Pleistocene epoch   period of geological history from about 2 million years ago to the present, when surges of glacial ice have been well documented

Pliocene   period of geological history from about 12 to 2 million years ago when PLATE interactions along the Pacific coast began

pluvial lake   lake which experiences a significant increase in depth due to increased precipitation or decreased evaporation

Precambrian   epoch of geological history from about 4 billion to 500 million years ago when the Earth formed as a planet, the crust developed, the first life-forms began in the sea, the first continental shield formed, and the first ever glaciation occurred; Precambrian rocks have been documented in the SHIELD areas of all of the continents by PALEOGEOLOGY

profundal   the deepest level of a lake or other body of water, consisting primarily of SEDIMENTS

pyroclastic flow   very fast, very hot flow of volcanic ash, gases, and air erupting from a volcano; fatal to everything in its path

Quaternary geology   the study of the PLEISTOCENE and HOLOCENE periods of Earth's history

rainshadow   the phenomenon in which the leeward side of a mountain or mountain range is starved of rain and snow since the windward side (usually the west side) receives virtually all the precipitation (as the mountains themselves block air masses causing them to rise and cool, producing rain there)

rift valley an area where FAULTING has caused a rift or trough in a crustal PLATE; can form the basin of a lake or a new ocean

Ring of Fire the edge of all the landmasses touching the Pacific Ocean, where TECTONIC ACTIVITY is intense since PLATE interactions are sustained

salinity saltiness of a body of water

saltpans dry, flat, low areas where natural salts have accumulated in the ground

Secchi disk white, flat circle-shaped geological tool attached to a thin rope which is marked as a measuring stick; lowered into a lake or pond until it becomes invisible, it thus establishes water clarity at depth

sediments the loose layers of soils, sands, muds, rocks, and decaying organisms that lie, for example, on the bottom of a body of water

seismic/seismic profiling geological technique in which energy waves are directed down into deep water and/or rock to discern what is there

shield the immense shield-shaped layer of ancient, often PRECAMBRIAN rock that lies in the inner areas of continents; is TECTONICALLY stable; also called CRATON

Silurian period of geological history from about 460 to 400 million years ago, when the earliest coral reefs formed in the sea

subduction zone area where an oceanic PLATE moves towards the lower crust as the result of a collision with a continental plate; causes earthquakes and volcanoes, as along the RING OF FIRE

submersible a very small submarine or "pod" built to withstand the immense water pressure deep down in a lake or ocean and equipped for scientific study

syncline downfolding and compression of rock layers

tectonic, tectonic activity, tectonic forces, tectonic plates related to the large-scale forces that move and shape extensive areas of the Earth's CRUST over long periods of time; examples: volcanoes, earthquakes, SUBDUCTION ZONES, FAULTING, mountain-building; caused by large plumes of seething MAGMA below the crust

tektites rocks which have been severely stressed or deformed by TECTONIC ACTIVITY, e.g., a rock that incorporates a glassy area as a result of a volcanic eruption

terrain any piece or area of land

terrane a piece or area of land defined by its geological nature

thermohaline referring to the heat and saltwater forces that guide the large-scale water currents of the planet, such as the Gulf Stream

Triassic the period of geological history from about 225 to 170 million years ago, when TECTONIC ACTIVITY was common in the eastern United States

volcanism volcanic activity

watershed area surrounding a given body of water in which all surface drainage is into that body of water; can be up to hundreds of thousands of square miles.

zooplankton the small animals that inhabit a lake or other body of water

Books

Chernicoff, Stanley, and Donna Whitney. *Geology: An Introduction to Physical Geology*. Boston, New York: Houghton Mifflin Company, 2002. An excellent introductory, college-level textbook.

Erickson, Jon. *The Living Earth: Making of the Earth*. New York: Facts On File, 2001. For high school students, an introduction to the principles of geology.

———. *The Living Earth: Rock Formations and Unusual Geologic Structures*. New York: Checkmark Books, 2001. Another in the excellent series, as the above title.

Gribbin, John, and Mary Gribbin. *Ice Age*. New York: Barnes & Noble Books, 2001. Short but very detailed about the geological background of ice ages past and future.

Harmon, Rick. *Crater Lake National Park, a History*. Corvallis: Oregon State University Press, 2002. Includes some national political and Native American history in addition to a clear description of the geology of this lake.

Levin, Harold L. *The Earth through Time*. Philadelphia: Saunders College Publishing, 1983. Though an older textbook, it includes good material additional to the first source.

Mackenzie, Fred T., and Judith A. Mackenzie *Our Changing Planet: An Introduction to Earth System Science and Global Environmental Change*. Upper Saddle River, N.J.: Prentice Hall, 1997. An excellent overview of the processes of geology on Earth.

McPhee, John. *Basin and Range*. New York: Farrar, Straus, & Giroux, 1980. Describes the geology of the western United States.

Melack, J. M., ed. *Saline Lakes*. Dordrecht, Netherlands: DRW. Junk, 1988. A monograph on these unusual lakes.

Serruya, Colette, and Utsa Pollingher. *Lakes of The Warm Belt*. Cambridge: Cambridge University Press, 1983. Useful, since most major lakes of the planet are not in the warmer areas and so are not treated in great detail by other sources.

Time Almanac 2004. Needham, Mass.: Pearson Education, 2003. Great for basic facts and lists, on this subject and others.

Wetzel, Robert G. *Limnology, Lake and River Ecosystems, Third Edition.* San Diego, Calif.: Academic Press, 2001. Very detailed information on the study of water bodies.

World Atlas, Millennium Edition. New York: DK Publishing, 1999. Another useful source for basic facts and lists.

Wyckoff, Jerome. *Reading the Earth, Landforms in the Making.* Mahwah, N.J.: Adastra West, 1999. Excellent in showing how visible landforms provide hints about ancient geological times.

Web Sites

Aral Sea Homepage
http://www.dfd.dlr.de/app/land/aralsee.
Contains written information, images, charts, etc.

Crater Lake National Park
http://www.nps.gov/crla/home.htm.
*The U.S. National Park Service's homepage for Crater Lake and its sur-
rounding park.*

**DOSECC (Drilling, Observation, and Sampling of the Earth's Conti-
nental Crust)**
http://www.dosecc.org.
*The site of a crustal drilling organization with specific information on the
geology at Lake Titicaca and Great Salt Lake.*

Glaciers, Glaciations, Ice Sheets, and Glacial Lakes
http://vulcan.usgs.gov/glossary/glaciers/framework.html.
*Information about glaciers as well as links to Ice Age information and facts
about volcanic lakes.*

Global Nature Foundation
http://www.globalnature.org.
*This German organization works to "save the lakes of the world" and pro-
vides many links and information about its efforts, with an emphasis
on European lakes.*

Google Scholar
http://www.scholar.google.com.
*This newest resource from Google provides access to the most up-to-date,
serious research findings on the subjects sought.*

The Great Lakes: Superior
http://www.great-lakes.net/lakes/superior.html.
This site contains all sorts of scientific and historical information about all the Great lakes, this page in particular being on Superior. It also contains links to other relevant government and university sites relating to Lake Superior.

International Hydrological Programme
http://www.unesco.org/water/ihp.
UNESCO's (United Nations Educational, Scientific and Cultural Organization) intergovernmental scientific program in water resources.

International Lake Environment Committee
http://www.ilec.or.jp/database/database.html.
An international lakes group that maintains a database on many of the world's lakes.

Lake Baikal Information Center
http://www.gran.baikal.net.
Part of the living lakes organization based at Lake Baikal, this site provides all sorts of information on this lake.

Lake Eyre Basin Coordinating Group
http://www.lakeeyrebasin.org/au.
All about Lake Eyre and its huge drainage area.

LakeNet
http://www.worldlakes.org.
A global network "working for the conservation and sustainable management of lakes." Based in the United States and working with organizations in 90 countries, the site has a lake search engine and provides information about lakes of the world, including many from the book.

Living Lakes Project
http://www.livinglakes.com.
An international lakes group, with information on world lakes including several from this book.

NASA's Visible Earth
http://earthobservatory.nasa.gov.
A searchable database of from-space images; many of the lakes can be seen here as from orbit. Extended information and photographs are offered for some of the lakes, such as the Caspian Sea, where extra sedimentation is shown in photographs and discussed.

The Science of Volcanic Lakes

http://lawr.ucdavis.edu/faculty/gpast/lakes.html.

This page from the Land, Air, and Water Resources department of the University of California-Davis "contains information on how volcanic lakes work and details about many specific lakes." It also contains pictures, diagrams, and charts.

SciTechResources.gov

http://www.scitechresources.gov.

A catalog of U.S. government science and technology Web sites with access to charts, graphs, reports, and databases.

Sea Grant

http://www.nsgo.seagrant.org.

Research program under the National Oceanographic and Atmospheric Administration that conducts research on the Great Lakes.

USGS Coastal and Marine Geology Program

http://marine.usgs.gov.

With articles on lakes featured in this book as well as many others.

USGS Water Resources

http://water.usgs.gov.

The United States Geological Survey is the government agency in charge of surveying national geology.

Volcanolive.com

http://www.volcanolive.com.

Contains volcano news and information, many photographs, and "over 4,000 pages of volcano information."

Magazines and Journals

Note to readers: This bibliography of magazines and journals has been prepared in a different fashion than is typical, because it is designed to be especially educational for readers. Though every specific journal reference is available from the author, upon request, these are not detailed here—high school readers working online to research the geology of lakes in this volume may find newer references by the time the book appears. Instead, the author is hereby guiding readers to the best sources in general, including the top journals found most useful in writing this book and the best science periodicals, where the newest material is explained in context, weekly or monthly. These sources are prioritized, categorized, and described so that readers may learn from them. As a former high school teacher, the author believes that this kind of working bibliography will serve readers best.

Magazines for the general public, consulted regularly in the writing of this book, and worth looking at regularly, for those interested in geology or any other science:

Audubon
700 Broadway
New York, NY 10003
http://www.magazine.audubon.org
Not only on birds, this magazine also covers various issues as they relate to the environment.

Discover
114 Fifth Avenue
New York, NY 10011
http://www.discover.com
An excellent monthly science magazine for the general public.

New Scientist
6277 Sea Harbor Drive
Orlando, FL 32887
http://www.newscientist.com
Covers the latest top research news in all fields of science.

Science News
1719 N Street, NW
Washington, DC 20036
http://www.sciencenews.org
Covers the latest top research news in all fields of science.

Magazines for the general public, consulted occasionally in the writing of this book and worth looking through occasionally for those interested in geology or any other science:

Australian Geographic
P.O. Box 321
Terrey Hills NSW 2084
Australia
http://editorial.australiangeographic.com.au
Covers visible geologic features in its area.

Canadian Geographic
39 McArthur Avenue
Ottawa, ON
Canada K1L 8L7
http://www.canadiangeographic.ca
Covers visible geologic features in its area.

Earth Island Journal
300 Broadway, Suite 28
San Francisco, CA 94133-3312
http://www.earthisland.org/eijournal/journal.cfm
Covers environmental geology issues.

Earthwatch
3 Clock Tower Place, Suite 100
Box 75
Maynard, MA 01754
http://www.earthwatch.org
Takes readers to research sites around the world and describes them in detail.

The Economist
111 West 57th Street
New York, NY 10019
http://www.economist.com
A general interest news magazine published in England.

Harper's Magazine
666 Broadway, 11th Floor
New York, NY 10012
http://www.harpers.org
A thoughtful general magazine with occasional articles on geologic issues.

The Lancet
360 Park Avenue South
New York, NY 10010-1710
http://www.thelancet.com
A top medical journal, with occasional pieces on environmental health.

Maclean's
One Mount Pleasant Road, 11th floor
Toronto, ON
M4Y 2Y5
Canada
http://www.macleans.ca
A general interest magazine published in Canada.

National Geographic
1145 17th Street NW
Washington, DC 20036-4688
http://nationalgeographic.com/ngm
Covers visible geologic features in the United States.

Naturalist
1427 East 60th Street
Chicago, IL 60637-2954
http://www.journals.uchicago.edu/AN/home.html
A natural history magazine with occasional geology articles.

Newsweek
251 West 57th Street
New York, NY 10019
http://www.msnbc.msn.com/id/3032542/site/newsweek/
A general interest news magazine.

Time
1271 Avenue of the Americas
New York, NY 10020
http://www.time.com
A general interest news magazine.

U.S. News & World Report
1050 Thomas Jefferson Street, NW
Washington, DC 20007
http://www.usnews.com
A general interest news magazine.

Index

Note: *Italic* page numbers indicate illustrations.
C indicates color insert pages.